P9-DIE-136

# *Practical* SHOP MATH

## SIMPLE SOLUTIONS TO WORKSHOP FRACTIONS, FORMULAS + GEOMETRIC SHAPES

WITHDRAWN

Text © 2006, 2018 by Tom Begnal

First edition published by F&W Publications under the title *Popular Woodworking Practical Shop Math* in 2006. Updated edition published by Spring House Press in 2018.

All rights reserved. No part of this book may be reproduced or transmitted in any form or by any means, electric or mechanical, including photocopying, recording, or by any information storage and retrieval system, without written permission from the Publisher.

The opinions expressed in this book are the author's own and do not necessarily reflect the views of Spring House Press.

Publisher: Paul McGahren
Editorial Director: Matthew Teague
Editor: Kerri Grzybicki
Designer: Lindsay Hess
Layout Designer: Jodie Delohery
Illustrator: Carolyn Mosher
Indexer: Jay Kreider

Cover photograph by Alex Kosev/Shutterstock.com

Spring House Press
P.O. Box 239
Whites Creek, TN 37189

ISBN: 978-1-940611-63-1

Library of Congress Control Number: 2018962958

Printed in The United States of America

10 9 8 7 6 5 4 3 2 1

Note: The following list contains names used in *Practical Shop Math* that may be registered with the United States Copyright Office: Formica; Plexiglas; The National Particleboard Association; The Woodbin (Sagulator); U.S. Forest Products Laboratory.

The information in this book is given in good faith; however, no warranty is given, nor are results guaranteed. Woodworking is inherently dangerous. Your safety is your responsibility. Neither Spring House Press nor the author assumes any responsibility for any injuries or accidents.

To learn more about Spring House Press books, or to find a retailer near you, email info@springhousepress.com or visit us at www.springhousepress.com.

# Practical SHOP MATH

## SIMPLE SOLUTIONS TO WORKSHOP FRACTIONS, FORMULAS + GEOMETRIC SHAPES

*Tom Begnal*

SPRING HOUSE PRESS

# CONTENTS

# INTRODUCTION

By its very nature, woodworking is a craft that requires a basic understanding of math. After all, you use various numbers—in the form of thickness, width and length dimensions—to describe the physical size of a woodworking project and its component parts. Inevitably, many of those dimensions—written as whole numbers, fractions and decimals—must be added, subtracted, multiplied and divided in order to cut and assemble a project.

Although math is an important part of woodworking, a surprising number of woodworkers feel somewhat intimidated when working with things like fractions, decimals, geometry, formulas and other math-related exercises. However, woodshop math is not something to be feared and avoided; it simply involves understanding and applying some basic information.

*Practical Shop Math* provides much of that information. The book shows, in an easy-to-understand format, how to work with fractions and decimals, powers and roots, shop geometry and compound angles. It also details how to enlarge grid patterns, solve right triangles, convert photos into dimensioned drawings and apply a number of useful formulas. Much of the information is presented in step-by-step format. In addition, a number of valuable conversion charts and an extensive table of powers and roots are included.

I hope you find that *Practical Shop Math* takes much of the mystery out of woodshop math. Once the mystery is gone, math becomes a lot easier and more enjoyable, and you'll become a better woodworker.

# Part One

# BASIC WOODSHOP ARITHMETIC

*A review of fractions, decimals, powers and roots*

CHAPTER 1

# Understanding Fractions

In the woodshop, you often need to work with part of a whole. For example, you might need to use part of a quart of polyurethane, not the whole quart; part of an inch, not the whole inch; part of a box of 100 screws, not the whole box of 100 screws; or part of a 4'-long pine board, not the whole board.

Before you can start doing any heavy lifting with fractions (like adding, subtracting, multiplying and dividing them), you need to understand some fraction basics. This chapter covers the fundamentals, so let's get started.

## What Is a Fraction?

In short, a *fraction* is a part of a whole. As an example, let's say you cut a 4'-long board into four 1'-long pieces (Fig. 1-1). (To simplify things, we are going to forget about saw-kerf waste.) Let's also say you use two of the four 1' lengths as drawer fronts for a hutch cupboard you are building.

Fig. 1-1

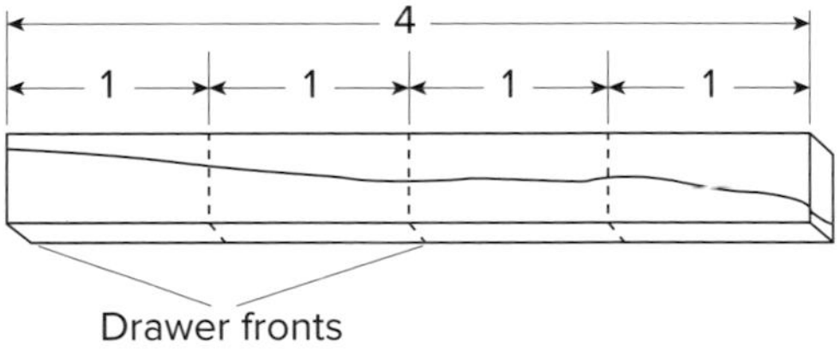


When you use two of the four 1' lengths, you have used two parts of the whole. Written as a fraction, it looks like this:

$$\frac{2}{4}$$

Note that the fraction is made up of two parts. The bottom part is called the *denominator,* while the top part is called the *numerator*. The line between the denominator and numerator is called the *fraction line* or *fraction bar*. Sometimes the fraction line is shown as a slanted line: $2/4$.

In any fraction, the denominator represents the number of equal parts that the whole has been divided into (4 in our board example), while the numerator represents the number of equal parts taken from the denominator (2 in our example).

## Reading Fractions

When reading a fraction, you read the numerator first, followed by the denominator.

Here is a list of some fractions commonly encountered in the workshop.

$1/2$ = one-half, $2/2$ = two-halves

$1/3$ = one-third, $2/3$ = two-thirds, $3/3$ = three-thirds

$1/4$ = one-quarter, $2/4$ = two-quarters, $3/4$ = three-quarters, etc.

$1/5$ = one-fifth, $2/5$ = two-fifths, $3/5$ = three-fifths, etc.

$1/6$ = one-sixth, $2/6$ = two-sixths, $3/6$ = three-sixths, etc.

$1/7$ = one-seventh, $2/7$ = two-sevenths, $3/7$ = three-sevenths, etc.

$1/8$ = one-eighth, $2/8$ = two-eighths, $3/8$ = three-eighths, etc.

$1/9$ = one-ninth, $2/9$ = two-ninths, $3/9$ = three ninths, etc.

$1/10$ = one-tenth, $2/10$ = two-tenths, $3/10$ = three-tenths, etc.

$\frac{1}{12}$ = one-twelfth, $\frac{2}{12}$ = two-twelfths, $\frac{3}{12}$ = three-twelfths, etc.
$\frac{1}{16}$ = one-sixteenth, $\frac{2}{16}$ = two-sixteenths, $\frac{3}{16}$ = three-sixteenths, etc.
$\frac{1}{32}$ = one-thirty-second, $\frac{2}{32}$ = two-thirty-seconds, etc.
$\frac{1}{64}$ = one-sixty-fourth, $\frac{2}{64}$ = two-sixty-fourths, etc.

## Fractions and Division

The symbol ÷ and the division box ( $\overline{)\phantom{--}}$ ) are used to indicate division. The fraction bar is also an indicator of division. Therefore, the fraction ¾ also means 2 ÷ 4.

## Types of Fractions

All fractions can be classified as either *proper fractions* or *improper fractions*.

### Proper Fractions

Proper fractions have a numerator that is smaller than the denominator. Examples of proper fractions are: ⅛, ⅜, ¾, ⁷⁄₁₆, ³¹⁄₃₂ and ²³⁄₆₄. The value of a proper fraction is always less than one. Put another way, if the denominator is divided into the numerator, the result is always less than one.

### Improper Fractions

Improper fractions have a numerator that is equal to or greater than the denominator. Examples of improper fractions are ²⁄₂, ³⁄₂, ⁴⁄₃, ²³⁄₈, ¹⁶⁄₁₆ and ⁶⁷⁄₆₄. The value of an improper fraction is always equal to or greater than one. That means if the denominator is divided into the numerator, the result is always equal to or greater than one.

## Reducing Fractions to Lowest Terms

The numerator and denominator of a fraction are called the *terms* of the fraction. When working with a fraction, it is often helpful to write the fraction in its lowest terms. You'll find that a fraction in its lowest terms is usually easier to use.

A fraction written in its lowest terms is called a *reduced fraction* and is said to be in its *simplest form*. The procedure for reducing a fraction to its lowest terms is sometimes called *simplifying* a fraction.

Let's look again at our example using the 4'-long board (Fig. 1-2). As you can see from the illustration, ¾ of the board is also equal to ½. Changing ¾ to ½ reduces the fraction to its lowest terms, although the value of the fraction remains the same.

Fig. 1-2

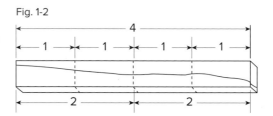

Let's look at another example and consider a 12'-long board that's cut into 1' lengths (Fig. 1-3). If you use four of the twelve 1' lengths, you have used four parts of the whole. Written as a fraction, it looks like this:

$$\frac{4}{12}$$

But as the illustration shows, the fraction ⁴⁄₁₂ is also equal to ⅓. Changing ⁴⁄₁₂ to ⅓ reduces the fraction to its lowest terms, yet the value remains the same: ⁴⁄₁₂ of the board is the same as ⅓ of the board.

While an illustration is handy for helping us see how a fraction can be reduced to lowest terms, it's not the most practical method for doing the work. Let's use some examples to show you another way.

Fig. 1-3

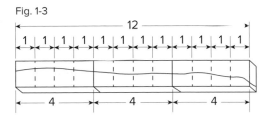

**EXAMPLE 1:** *Reduce the fraction ⁶⁄₈ to lowest terms.*

**Step 1:** Look at the fraction and determine the largest number that divides evenly into both the numerator and denominator. Usually, this step takes some guessing and bit of trial and error.

For this example, my thinking goes something like this: Both terms are even numbers, so I know 2 is a possibility. But is there a number larger than 2 that will divide evenly into both terms? The numbers 3 and 6 divide into the numerator (6) but not into the denominator (8). The number 4 divides into the denominator (8), but not the numerator (6). The numbers 5 and 7 won't divide evenly into either term, so 2 is the number.

**Step 2:** Divide the numerator and denominator by 2.

$$\frac{6 \div 2}{8 \div 2} = \frac{3}{4}$$

The fraction ⁶⁄₈ reduced to the lowest terms is ¾.

**EXAMPLE 2:** *Reduce the fraction ²¹⁄₃₀ to lowest terms.*

**Step 1:** Look at the fraction and determine the largest number that divides evenly into both the numerator and denominator. The numerator is not an even number, so neither 2 nor any even number is a possibility. The number 3 divides evenly into both the numerator (21) and the denominator (30), so it is a possibility. The numbers 5, 9, 11, 13, 15, 17 and 19 won't divide into the numerator (21), and the number 7 won't divide into the denominator, so 3 is the number.

**Step 2:** Divide the numerator and denominator by 3.

$$\frac{21 \div 3}{30 \div 3} = \frac{7}{10}$$

The fraction ²¹⁄₃₀ reduced to lowest terms is ⁷⁄₁₀.

**EXAMPLE 3:** *Reduce the fraction ⁹⁄₁₆ to lowest terms.*

**Step 1:** Look at the fraction and determine the largest number that divides evenly into both the numerator and denominator. The numerator is not an even number, so even numbers are not candidates. The number 3 divides evenly into the numerator (9) but not the denominator (16). The numbers 5 and 7 won't divide into either term. The number 9 divides into the numerator (9) but not the denominator (16). Therefore, the fraction ⁹⁄₁₆ cannot be reduced to lower terms.

## Raising Fractions to Higher Terms

When working with fractions, it is sometimes necessary to raise a fraction to higher terms. The procedure is pretty straightforward: You simply multiply both the numerator and denominator by a *common number*, sometimes called a *common multiplier*. Let's use the fraction ⅝ and a common number of 4.

$$\frac{5 \times 4}{8 \times 4} = \frac{20}{32}$$

Indeed, you can multiply the numerator and denominator by any common number and the fraction will be raised to higher terms.

$$\frac{5 \times 2}{8 \times 2} = \frac{10}{16} \text{ and } \frac{5 \times 6}{8 \times 6} = \frac{30}{48} \text{ and } \frac{5 \times 21}{8 \times 21} = \frac{105}{168}$$

## Equivalent Fractions

We now know that when a fraction is reduced to its lowest terms (for example, ⁴⁄₆ to ⅔), the original and reduced fractions have the same value. We also know that when a fraction is raised to higher terms (for example, ¼ to ³⁄₁₂), the original and raised fraction also have the same value. Fractions that have the same value are called *equivalent fractions*. The fractions ½, ²⁄₄, ⁴⁄₈, ⁸⁄₁₆, ¹⁶⁄₃₂ and ³²⁄₆₄ are examples of equivalent fractions because they all have the same value.

## Making a Whole Number a Fraction

You can turn any whole number into a fraction. To do it, simply write the whole number as the numerator and write the number 1 as the denominator. For example, to make the number 7 a fraction, write 7 as the numerator and 1 as the denominator. The fraction looks like this:

$$\frac{7}{1}$$

Here are a few more examples:

| Whole Number | Whole Number as a Fraction |
|---|---|
| 1 | ¹⁄₁ |
| 5 | ⁵⁄₁ |
| 14 | ¹⁴⁄₁ |
| 137 | ¹³⁷⁄₁ |

## Common Denominators

When doing certain operations—like adding and subtracting—with two or more fractions, all the fractions must have the same denominator. Fractions with the same denominator are said to have a *common denominator*. More specifically, a common denominator is a number that is evenly divisible by the denominators of all fractions you are using. Let's look at an example.

**EXAMPLE 1:** *Find a common denominator for the fractions ⅓ and ⁴⁄₉, then write the equivalent fractions using the common denominator.*

**Step 1:** If possible, reduce one or both of the fractions to lowest terms. In this case, neither fraction can be reduced.

**Step 2:** To produce a common denominator, multiply the denominator of one fraction times the denominator of the second: 3 × 9 = 27. Therefore, a common denominator for these fractions is 27.

**Step 3:** Raise both fractions to higher terms using the common denominator. To raise ⅓ to higher terms with a denominator of 27, use 9 as the common denominator.

$$\frac{1 \times 9}{3 \times 9} = \frac{9}{27}$$

To raise ⁴⁄₉ to higher terms with a denominator of 27, use 3 as the common number.

$$\frac{4 \times 3}{9 \times 3} = \frac{12}{27}$$

The number 27 is a common denominator for the fractions ⅓ and ⁴⁄₉. The equivalent fractions are ⁹⁄₂₇ (for ⅓) and ¹²⁄₂₇ (for ⁴⁄₉).

## Lowest Common Denominator

It's not unusual for two or more fractions to have more than one common denominator. In the example we just looked at, in addition to the number 27, the numbers 9, 18, 36, 45 and 54 are some of the possible common denominators.

When working with fractions, it is sometimes easier to use the *lowest common denominator*, also called the *LCD*. The lowest common denominator is the smallest number that is evenly divisible by the denominators of all the fractions you are using. In the example we just did, the number 9 is the lowest common denominator. To find out how to find the LCD, let's look at a couple of examples.

**EXAMPLE 1:** *Find the lowest common denominator for the fractions ⅛ and ⁵⁄₆, then write the equivalent fractions using that denominator.*

**Step 1:** If possible, reduce one or both of the fractions to lowest terms. In this case, neither fraction can be reduced.

**Step 2:** Next, check to see if the largest denominator (8 in our example) can serve as the lowest common denominator for the fractions. It can't, so you must do some more looking.

The process of finding the LCD takes a bit of trial and error. You know that you can find a common denominator simply by multiplying the two denominators (8 × 6 = 48). But in this case, you want the lowest common denominator, which might or might not be 48.

To find the LCD, begin by multiplying the largest denominator (8) by 2: 8 × 2 = 16. Check to see if both denominators divide evenly into 16. Since 8 does and 6 doesn't, multiply the largest denominator by 3: 8 × 3 = 24. Do both denominators divide evenly into 24? Bingo, they do, so the lowest common denominator is 24.

**Step 3:** Raise the fractions to higher terms with the lowest common denominator. To raise ⅛ to a higher term that has a denominator of 24, use 3 as the common number.

$$\frac{1 \times 3}{8 \times 3} = \frac{3}{24}$$

To raise ⁵⁄₆ to a higher term that has a denominator of 24, use 4 as the common number.

$$\frac{5 \times 4}{6 \times 4} = \frac{20}{24}$$

The number 24 is the lowest common denominator for the fractions ⅛ and ⅚. The equivalent fractions are ³⁄₂₄ and ²⁰⁄₂₄.

**EXAMPLE 2:** *Find the lowest common denominator for the fractions ²⁄₆, ³⁄₈ and ⁷⁄₁₂, then write the equivalent fractions using that denominator.*

**Step 1:** If possible, reduce the fractions to lowest terms. In this case, the fraction ²⁄₆ can be reduced.

$$\frac{2 \div 2}{6 \div 2} = \frac{1}{3}$$

The new fraction group is now ⅓, ³⁄₈ and ⁷⁄₁₂.

**Step 2:** Check to see if the largest denominator (12 in this example) can serve as the lowest common denominator for all three fractions. It can't, so you must keep looking.

You can find a common denominator simply by multiplying the three denominators ($3 \times 8 \times 12 = 288$), but you are looking for the lowest common denominator, which might or might not be 288.

To find the LCD, begin by multiplying the largest denominator (12) by 2: $12 \times 2 = 24$. See if the other two denominators divide evenly into 24. They do, so the lowest common denominator is 24.

**Step 3:** Raise the fractions to higher terms with the lowest common denominator. To raise ⅓ to a higher term that has a denominator of 24, use 8 as the common number.

$$\frac{1 \times 8}{3 \times 8} = \frac{8}{24}$$

To raise ³⁄₈ to higher terms with a denominator of 24, use 3 as the common number.

$$\frac{3 \times 3}{8 \times 3} = \frac{9}{24}$$

To raise ⁷⁄₁₂ to higher terms with a denominator of 24, use 2 as the common number.

$$\frac{7 \times 2}{12 \times 2} = \frac{14}{24}$$

The number 24 is the lowest common denominator for the fractions ²⁄₆, ³⁄₈ and ⁷⁄₁₂. The equivalent fractions are ⁸⁄₂₄, ⁹⁄₂₄ and ¹⁴⁄₂₄.

## Like Fractions and Unlike Fractions

Fractions with a common denominator are called *like fractions*. The fractions ¹⁄₁₆, ³⁄₁₆, ⁸⁄₁₆, ¹²⁄₁₆ and ¹⁵⁄₁₆ are examples of like fractions because they all have the number 16 as a denominator.

Fractions with different denominators are called *unlike fractions*. The fractions ¾, ³⁄₈, ⁹⁄₁₆ and ¹²⁄₃₂ are examples of unlike fractions.

### Comparing Like Fractions

When fractions have a common denominator, it's easy to determine which one is bigger. For example, let's say you have a pair of 1-gallon containers partially filled with wood stain; one is ⅝ full and the other is ⅞ full. Which has more stain? When you have like fractions the answer is easy: the fractions with the larger numerator always represents the larger fraction—in this case ⅞.

## Comparing Unlike Fractions

Let's say we find a couple more 1-gallon containers partially filled with stain. One is ¾ full; the other is ⁹⁄₁₆ full. Which one has more stain?

In this case, the fractions are unlike, so you can't simply compare the numerators to find out which container has the most stain. Instead, you must convert one or both fractions so they have a common denominator; then you can compare the numerators.

First, if possible, reduce the fractions to lowest terms. This step usually makes the next steps easier. In this case, however, both fractions are already at their lowest terms.

Next, check to see if the larger denominator (16 in our example) can serve as a common denominator for both fractions. If it can, it's going to save some work. In this case, the denominator of 4 can be divided into 16, which means the fraction ¾ can be raised to higher terms with 16 as the denominator.

Now, raise the fraction ¾ to higher terms so the equivalent fraction has a denominator of 16. Using a common number of 4 produces a denominator of 16.

$$\frac{3 \times 4}{4 \times 4} = \frac{12}{16}$$

With the denominators the same, you are able to compare the fractions in question: ¹²⁄₁₆ and ⁹⁄₁₆. As discussed earlier, when you have like fractions, the fraction with the larger numerator always represents the larger fraction—in this case, ¹²⁄₁₆. Therefore, the container that's ¾ full has more stain.

Let's look at one more example and use a step-by-step procedure to determine which is bigger: ¼ or ⁴⁄₆.

**Step 1:** If possible, reduce the fractions to lowest terms. Looking at the two fractions here, you can see that the fraction ¼ can't be reduced. However, ⁴⁄₆ can be reduced by dividing both the numerator and denominator by 2.

$$\frac{4 \div 2}{6 \div 2} = \frac{2}{3}$$

Now let's compare the fractions ¼ and ⅔.

**Step 2:** Next, check to see if the larger denominator (4 in our example) can serve as a common denominator for the fractions. Since it can't, you must find a common denominator, so multiply the denominator of one fraction by the denominator of the second: 4 × 3 = 12. Therefore, a common denominator for both fractions is 12.

**Step 3:** Raise the fractions to higher terms with 12 as a denominator. To raise ¼ to higher terms with a denominator of 12, use 3 as the common number.

$$\frac{1 \times 3}{4 \times 3} = \frac{3}{12}$$

To raise ⅔ to higher terms with a denominator of 12, use 4 as the common number.

$$\frac{2 \times 4}{3 \times 4} = \frac{8}{12}$$

**Step 4:** Compare the like fractions ³⁄₁₂ and ⁸⁄₁₂. The fraction ⁸⁄₁₂ is greater than ³⁄₁₂. Therefore, ⁴⁄₆ is greater than ¼.

## Mixed Numbers

Sometimes a whole number is combined with a fraction. A number that contains both a whole number and a proper fraction is called a *mixed number*. Examples of mixed numbers are 1¼, 5⅞, 12½ and 47¹⁷⁄₃₂.

Mixed numbers are directly related to improper fractions. Indeed, mixed numbers can be converted easily to improper fractions, and improper fractions can be changed easily to mixed numbers.

### Changing Improper Fractions to Mixed Numbers

You will recall that the fraction line is an indicator of division. In division, the number to be divided is called the *dividend*, while the number by which we divide is called the *divisor*. The number that results is called the *quotient*.

Changing an improper fraction to a mixed number is pretty simple: You need only divide the numerator. Let's look at a couple of examples:

**EXAMPLE 1:** *Change the improper fraction ⁹⁄₂ to a mixed number.*

**Step 1:** Divide 9 by 2.

$$
\begin{array}{r}
4 \\
2\overline{)\,9} \\
8 \\
\hline
1 \quad \text{(remainder)}
\end{array}
$$

**Step 2:** Write the quotient as a whole number (4), then write the remainder (1) and divisor (2) as a fraction, with the remainder as the numerator and the divisor as the denominator. If necessary, reduce the fraction to its lowest terms.

$$
\begin{array}{r}
4 = 4\frac{1}{2} \\
2\overline{)\,9} \\
8 \\
\hline
1 \quad \text{(remainder)}
\end{array}
$$

The fraction ½ is already at its lowest terms. Therefore, the improper fraction ⁹⁄₂ equals the mixed number 4½.

**EXAMPLE 2:** *Change the improper fraction ²⁶⁄₈ to a mixed number.*

**Step 1:** Divide 26 by 8.

$$
\begin{array}{r}
3 \\
8\overline{)\,26} \\
24 \\
\hline
2 \quad \text{(remainder)}
\end{array}
$$

**Step 2:** Write the quotient as a whole number (3), then write the remainder (2) and divisor (8) as a fraction, with the remainder as the numerator and the divisor as the denominator. If necessary, reduce the fraction to its lowest terms.

$$
\begin{array}{r}
3 = 3\frac{2}{8} \\
8\overline{)\,26} \\
24 \\
\hline
2 \quad \text{(remainder)}
\end{array}
$$

Reduce the fraction ⅝ to its lowest terms.

$$
\frac{2 \div 2}{8 \div 2} = \frac{1}{4}
$$

The improper fraction ²⁶⁄₈ equals the mixed number 3¼ .

## Changing Mixed Numbers to Improper Fractions

When working with fractions, you'll sometimes need to change a mixed number to an improper fraction. Here are a few examples that show how to do it.

**EXAMPLE 1:** *Convert 4⅔ to an improper fraction.*

Create a new numerator by multiplying the denominator of the fraction (3) by the whole number (4) then adding the numerator of the fraction (2). The denominator remains the same.

$$4\tfrac{2}{3} = \frac{(3 \times 4) + 2}{3} = \frac{12 + 2}{3} = \frac{14}{3}$$

The mixed number 4⅔ is equal to the fraction ¹⁴⁄₃.

**EXAMPLE 2:** *Convert 11⅝ to an improper fraction.*

As in Example 1, create a new numerator by multiplying the denominator of the fraction by the whole number then adding the numerator of the fraction. Keep the same denominator.

$$11\tfrac{5}{8} = \frac{(8 \times 11) + 5}{8} = \frac{88 + 5}{8} = \frac{93}{8}$$

The mixed number 11⅝ is equal to the fraction ⁹³⁄₈.

CHAPTER 2

# Working with Fractions

Fractions seem to be as much a part of woodworking as a well-cut dovetail joint. Parts of things are constantly being added, subtracted, multiplied and divided. We add fractions of an inch, subtract fractions of a meter, multiply fractions of a pound and divide fractions of an angle. No doubt, a good understanding of how to work with fractions can make your time in the woodshop more productive. If fractions have intimidated you in the past, take heart. This chapter will show you how to solve just about any problem that involves a fraction.

## Adding Fractions

Addition is the most common operation involving fractions. The examples that follow show how to add like fractions, unlike fractions and mixed numbers.

### Adding Like Fractions

As you know, two or more fractions with a common denominator are called like fractions. The procedure for adding like fractions is pretty basic: you simply add all the numerators and write the sum over the common denominator. Then, if possible, reduce the new fraction to its lowest terms. Let's look at some examples.

**EXAMPLE 1:** *Add ⅛ and ⅜.*

**Step 1:** Write the problem.

$$\frac{1}{8} + \frac{3}{8} =$$

**Step 2:** Add all the numerators and write the numerator sum: 1 + 3 = 4.

$$\frac{1}{8} + \frac{3}{8} = \frac{4}{\rule{1cm}{0.4pt}} \text{ (numerator sum)}$$

**Step 3:** Write the common denominator (8) under the numerator sum.

$$\frac{1}{8} + \frac{3}{8} = \frac{4}{8} \text{ (common denominator)}$$

**Step 4:** If possible, reduce the sum to lowest terms.

$$\frac{4 \div 4}{8 \div 4} = \frac{1}{2}$$

Therefore, ⅛ + ⅜ = ½.

**EXAMPLE 2:** *Add ⁷⁄₁₂ and ⁵⁄₁₂.*

**Step 1:** Write the problem.

$$\frac{7}{12} + \frac{5}{12} =$$

**Step 2:** Add all the numerators and write the numerator sum: 7 + 5 = 12.

$$\frac{7}{12} + \frac{5}{12} = \frac{12}{\rule{1cm}{0.4pt}}$$

**Step 3:** Write the common denominator (12) under the numerator sum.

$$\frac{7}{12} + \frac{5}{12} = \frac{12}{12}$$

**Step 4:** If possible, reduce the sum to lowest terms. From chapter one, you know that any number divided by itself is equal to 1.

$$\frac{12}{12} = 1$$

Therefore, $\frac{7}{12} + \frac{5}{12} = 1$.

**EXAMPLE 3:** *Add* $\frac{5}{16}$, $\frac{7}{16}$ *and* $\frac{9}{16}$.

**Step 1:** Write the problem.

$$\frac{5}{16} + \frac{7}{16} + \frac{9}{16} =$$

**Step 2:** Add all the numerators and write the numerator sum: 5 + 7 + 9 = 21.

$$\frac{5}{16} + \frac{7}{16} + \frac{9}{16} = \frac{21}{}$$

**Step 3:** Write the common denominator (16) under the numerator sum.

$$\frac{5}{16} + \frac{7}{16} + \frac{9}{16} = \frac{21}{16}$$

**Step 4:** Since the sum $\frac{21}{16}$ is an improper fraction, change the improper fraction to a mixed number (as described in chapter one).

$$\begin{array}{r} 1 \\ 16\overline{)21} \\ 16 \\ \hline 5 \text{ (remainder)} \end{array}$$

Therefore, $\frac{5}{16} + \frac{7}{16} + \frac{9}{16} = \frac{21}{16} = 1\frac{5}{16}$.

## Adding Mixed Numbers That Have Like Fractions

Mixed numbers that have like fractions are added in much the same way as like fractions. You add the whole numbers first, then add the like fractions. Let's look at a few examples.

**EXAMPLE 1:** *Add* $2\frac{3}{8}$ *and* $5\frac{1}{8}$.

**Step 1:** Write the problem.

$$2\frac{3}{8} + 5\frac{1}{8} =$$

**Step 2:** Add the whole numbers: 2 + 5 = 7.

$$2\frac{3}{8} + 5\frac{1}{8} = 7$$

**Step 3:** Add the numerators of the fractions: 3 + 1 = 4.

$$2\frac{3}{8} + 5\frac{1}{8} = 7\frac{4}{}$$

**Step 4:** Write the common denominator (8) under the numerator.

$$2\frac{3}{8} + 5\frac{1}{8} = 7\frac{4}{8}$$

**Step 5:** If possible, reduce the fraction to lowest terms.

$$\frac{4 \div 4}{8 \div 4} = \frac{1}{2}$$

Therefore, $2\frac{3}{8} + 5\frac{1}{8} = 7\frac{4}{8} = 7\frac{1}{2}$.

**EXAMPLE 2: *Add 3 $\frac{7}{16}$ and 5 $\frac{9}{16}$.***

**Step 1:** Write the problem.

$$3\tfrac{7}{16} + 5\tfrac{9}{16} =$$

**Step 2:** Add the whole numbers: 3 + 5 = 8.

$$3\tfrac{7}{16} + 5\tfrac{9}{16} = 8$$

**Step 3:** Add the fraction numerators: 7 + 9 = 16.

$$3\tfrac{7}{16} + 5\tfrac{9}{16} = 8\tfrac{16}{}$$

**Step 4:** Write the common denominator (16) under the numerator.

$$3\tfrac{7}{16} + 5\tfrac{9}{16} = 8\tfrac{16}{16}$$

**Step 5:** If possible, reduce the fraction to lowest terms. From chapter one, you know that any number divided by itself is equal to 1.

$$\frac{16}{16} = 1$$

**Step 6:** The reduced fraction produces a whole number of 1, so add the whole numbers: 8 + 1 = 9.

$$3\tfrac{7}{16} + 5\tfrac{9}{16} = 8\tfrac{16}{16} = 8 + 1 = 9$$

Therefore, $3\frac{7}{16} + 5\frac{9}{16} = 9$.

**EXAMPLE 3: *Add 6 $\frac{1}{8}$, 2 $\frac{5}{8}$ and 4 $\frac{7}{8}$.***

**Step 1:** Write the problem.

$$6\tfrac{1}{8} + 2\tfrac{5}{8} + 4\tfrac{7}{8} =$$

**Step 2:** Add the whole numbers: 6 + 2 + 4 = 12

$$6\tfrac{1}{8} + 2\tfrac{5}{8} + 4\tfrac{7}{8} = 12$$

**Step 3:** Add the fraction numerators: 1 + 5 + 7 = 13

$$6\tfrac{1}{8} + 2\tfrac{5}{8} + 4\tfrac{7}{8} = 12\tfrac{13}{}$$

**Step 4:** Write the common denominator (8) under the numerator.

$$6\tfrac{1}{8} + 2\tfrac{5}{8} + 4\tfrac{7}{8} = 12\tfrac{13}{8}$$

**Step 5:** Since the sum $\frac{13}{8}$ is an improper fraction, change the improper fraction to a mixed number.

$$\begin{array}{r} 1 \\ 8\overline{)13} \\ \underline{8} \\ 5 \end{array} \text{ (remainder)}$$

The improper fraction $13/8$ is equal to the mixed number $1\frac{5}{8}$.

**Step 6:** Add the whole number (12) and mixed number ($1\frac{5}{8}$).

$$12 + 1\tfrac{5}{8} = 13\tfrac{5}{8}$$

Therefore, $6\frac{1}{8} + 2\frac{5}{8} + 4\frac{7}{8} = 13\frac{5}{8}$.

## Adding Unlike Fractions

From chapter one, you know that unlike fractions are fractions that have different denominators. Unlike fractions can be added, but first they must be changed to fractions that have common denominators. (If necessary, review chapter one to see how to find a common denominator for unlike fractions.)  Let's look at an example.

**EXAMPLE: *Add ½ and ⅜.***

**Step 1:** Write the problem.

$$\frac{1}{2} + \frac{3}{8} =$$

**Step 2:** Determine the lowest common denominator. The lowest common denominator is 8.

**Step 3:** Raise the fraction ½ to higher terms with the common denominator 8, using 4 as the common number.

$$\frac{1 \times 4}{2 \times 4} = \frac{4}{8}$$

**Step 4:** Add the like fractions.

$$\frac{4}{8} + \frac{3}{8} = \frac{7}{8}$$

Therefore, $\frac{1}{2} + \frac{3}{8} = \frac{7}{8}$.

## Adding Mixed Numbers That Have Unlike Fractions

Mixed numbers that have unlike fractions are added in much the same way as unlike fractions. You convert the unlike fractions to like fractions before adding the whole numbers and the fractions. Let's look at an example.

**EXAMPLE: *Add 5³⁄₁₆ and 3¼.***

**Step 1:** Write the problem.

$$5\tfrac{3}{16} + 3\tfrac{1}{4} =$$

**Step 2:** Determine the lowest common denominator. The lowest common denominator is 16.

**Step 3:** Raise the fraction ¼ to higher terms with the common denominator 16, using 4 as the common number.

$$\frac{1 \times 4}{4 \times 4} = \frac{4}{16}$$

**Step 4:** Rewrite the problem.

$$5\tfrac{3}{16} + 3\tfrac{4}{16} =$$

**Step 5:** Add the whole numbers.

$$5\tfrac{3}{16} + 3\tfrac{4}{16} = 8$$

**Step 6:** Add the fractions.

$$5\tfrac{3}{16} + 3\tfrac{4}{16} = 8\tfrac{7}{16}$$

Therefore, $5\tfrac{3}{16} + 3\tfrac{1}{4} = 8\tfrac{7}{16}$

## Subtracting Fractions

Subtraction is probably the second most common operation involving fractions. The examples that follow show how to subtract like fractions, unlike fractions and mixed numbers.

### Subtracting Like Fractions

Subtracting like fractions is a pretty easy procedure. You simply subtract the numerators and write the sum over the common denominator. Then, if possible, reduce the new fraction to its lowest terms. Let's look at a couple of examples.

**EXAMPLE 1:** *Subtract ⅜ from ⅝.*

**Step 1:** Write the problem.

$$\frac{5}{8} - \frac{3}{8} =$$

**Step 2:** Subtract the numerators: 5 − 3 = 2.

$$\frac{5}{8} - \frac{3}{8} = \frac{2}{}$$

**Step 3:** Write the common denominator (8) under the difference.

$$\frac{5}{8} - \frac{3}{8} = \frac{2}{8}$$

**Step 4:** If possible, reduce the sum to lowest terms.

$$\frac{2 \div 2}{8 \div 2} = \frac{1}{4}$$

Therefore, $\tfrac{5}{8} - \tfrac{3}{8} = \tfrac{1}{4}$.

**EXAMPLE 2:** *Subtract ¹¹⁄₃₂ from ⁴⁵⁄₃₂.*

**Step 1:** Write the problem.

$$\frac{45}{32} - \frac{11}{32} =$$

**Step 2:** Subtract the numerators: 45 − 11 = 34.

$$\frac{45}{32} - \frac{11}{32} = \frac{34}{}$$

**Step 3:** Write the common denominator (32) under the difference.

$$\frac{45}{32} - \frac{11}{32} = \frac{34}{32}$$

**Step 4:** If possible, reduce to lowest terms.

$$\frac{34 \div 2}{32 \div 2} = \frac{17}{16}$$

**Step 5:** Change the improper fraction $^{17}/_{16}$ to a mixed number (if necessary, see chapter one for review).

$$\frac{17}{16} = 1\tfrac{1}{16}$$

Therefore, $^{45}/_{32} - ^{11}/_{32} = 1\tfrac{1}{16}$.

### Exchanging to Subtract Mixed Numbers with Like Fractions

Let's look at an example to see how to do this kind of subtraction.

**EXAMPLE:** *Subtract 4⅝ from 8⅜.*

**Step 1:** Write the problem.

$$8\tfrac{3}{8} - 4\tfrac{5}{8} =$$

**Step 2:** Subtract the numerators.
Since 5 is greater than 3, exchange the whole number 8 for the whole number 7 plus the fraction ⅜ (we know that 7 + ⅜ = 8). The problem now looks like this:

$$8\tfrac{3}{8} - 4\tfrac{5}{8} = (7\tfrac{8}{8} + \tfrac{3}{8}) - 4\tfrac{5}{8} = 7\tfrac{11}{8} - 4\tfrac{5}{8}$$

Now the numerators can be subtracted:
$11 - 5 = 6$.

$$7\tfrac{11}{8} - 4\tfrac{5}{8} = {}^{6}/$$

**Step 3:** Write the common denominator (8) under the numerator difference.

$$7\tfrac{11}{8} - 4\tfrac{5}{8} = {}^{6}/_{8}$$

**Step 4:** Subtract the whole numbers: $7 - 4 = 3$.

$$7\tfrac{11}{8} - 4\tfrac{5}{8} = 3\tfrac{6}{8}$$

**Step 5:** If possible, reduce the fraction to lowest terms.

$$\frac{6 \div 2}{8 \div 2} = \frac{3}{4}$$

Therefore, $8\tfrac{3}{8} - 4\tfrac{5}{8} = 3\tfrac{3}{4}$.

### Subtracting Unlike Fractions

Unlike fractions can be subtracted, but first they must be changed to fractions that have a common denominator. (If necessary, review chapter one to see how to find a common denominator for unlike fractions.)

**EXAMPLE:** *Subtract $^{5}/_{16}$ from ⅞.*

**Step 1:** Write the problem.

$$\frac{7}{8} - \frac{5}{16} =$$

**Step 2:** Determine the lowest common denominator. The lowest common denominator is 16.

**Step 3:** Raise the fraction ⅞ to higher terms with the common denominator 16, using 2 as the common number.

$$\frac{7 \times 2}{8 \times 2} = \frac{14}{16}$$

**Step 4:** Subtract the like fractions.

$$\frac{14}{16} - \frac{5}{16} = \frac{9}{16}$$

Therefore, $\frac{7}{8} - \frac{5}{16} = \frac{9}{16}$, which cannot be reduced.

## Exchanging to Subtract Mixed Numbers with Unlike Fractions

**EXAMPLE:** *Subtract 15 $\frac{11}{16}$ from 28 $\frac{5}{32}$.*

**Step 1:** Write the problem.

$$28\tfrac{5}{32} - 15\tfrac{11}{16} =$$

**Step 2:** Determine the lowest common denominator. The lowest common denominator is 32.

**Step 3:** Raise the fraction $\frac{11}{16}$ to higher terms with the common denominator 32, using 2 as the common number.

$$\frac{11 \times 2}{16 \times 2} = \frac{22}{32}$$

**Step 4:** Rewrite the problem with the common denominator.

$$28\tfrac{5}{32} - 15\tfrac{22}{32} =$$

**Step 5:** Subtract the numerators.
Since 22 is greater than 5, exchange the whole number 28 for the whole number 27 plus the fraction $\frac{32}{32}$ (we know that $27 + \frac{32}{32} = 28$). The problem now looks like this.

$$28\tfrac{5}{32} - 15\tfrac{22}{32} = (27\tfrac{32}{32} + \tfrac{5}{32}) - 15\tfrac{22}{32} = 27\tfrac{37}{32} - 15\tfrac{22}{32}$$

Now the numerators can be subtracted:
$37 - 22 = 15$.

$$27\tfrac{37}{32} - 15\tfrac{22}{32} = {}^{15}/$$

**Step 6:** Write the common denominator (32) under the numerator difference.

$$27\tfrac{37}{32} - 15\tfrac{22}{32} = \tfrac{15}{32}$$

**Step 7:** Subtract the whole numbers:
$27 - 15 = 12$.

$$27\tfrac{37}{32} - 15\tfrac{22}{32} = 12\tfrac{15}{32}$$

Therefore, $28\tfrac{5}{32} - 15\tfrac{11}{16} = 12\tfrac{15}{32}$.

## Multiplying Fractions

In the woodshop, there are plenty of opportunities to multiply fractions. The examples that follow show how to multiply a fraction by a fraction, a fraction by a whole number and a fraction by a mixed number.

### Multiplying a Fraction by a Fraction
To do this type of multiplication, you simply calculate numerator times numerator and denominator times denominator. Let's look at an example.

**EXAMPLE:** *Multiply ½ by $\frac{13}{16}$.*

**Step 1:** Write the problem.

$$\frac{1}{2} \times \frac{13}{16}$$

**Step 2:** Multiply the numerators.

$$\frac{1}{2} \times \frac{13}{16} = \frac{13}{}$$

**Step 3:** Multiply the denominators.

$$\frac{1}{2} \times \frac{13}{16} = \frac{13}{32}$$

**Step 4:** If possible, reduce the fraction to lowest terms. The fraction $^{13}/_{32}$ can't be reduced.

Therefore, $\frac{1}{2} \times \,^{13}/_{16} = \,^{13}/_{32}$.

## Canceling

Fraction multiplication can often be simplified by using a procedure called *canceling*. When it can be used, canceling effectively reduces the fractions to lower terms right from the start. This makes for easier multiplication and often eliminates the need to reduce the fraction at the end of the procedure. Let's look at an example.

**EXAMPLE:** *Multiply ⅖ by ¾.*

**Step 1:** Write the problem.

$$\frac{2}{5} \times \frac{3}{4}$$

**Step 2:** Cancel, if possible, by finding a common number that can divide evenly into any numerator and any denominator.

In this problem, the common number 2 divides into the numerator 2 and denominator 4.

$$\frac{\overset{1}{\cancel{2}}}{5} \times \frac{3}{\underset{2}{\cancel{4}}}$$

**Step 3:** Multiply the numerators.

$$\frac{\overset{1}{\cancel{2}}}{5} \times \frac{3}{\underset{2}{\cancel{4}}} = \frac{3}{}$$

**Step 4:** Multiply the denominators.

$$\frac{\overset{1}{\cancel{2}}}{5} \times \frac{3}{\underset{2}{\cancel{4}}} = \frac{3}{10}$$

This product $^{3}/_{10}$ can't be reduced; therefore, $\frac{2}{5} \times \frac{3}{4} = \,^{3}/_{10}$.

## Multiplying a Fraction by a Whole Number

Recall from chapter one that a whole number can be changed into a fraction by writing the whole number as the numerator and using 1 as the denominator.

**EXAMPLE:** *Multiply ¼ by 9.*

**Step 1:** Write the problem.

$$\frac{1}{4} \times \frac{9}{1}$$

**Step 2:** Cancel, if possible.
No common number besides 1 can divide evenly into both numerator and denominator; therefore, no cancellation can be done.

**Step 3:** Multiply the numerators.

$$\frac{1}{4} \times \frac{9}{1} = \frac{9}{\ }$$

**Step 4:** Multiply the denominators.

$$\frac{1}{4} \times \frac{9}{1} = \frac{9}{4}$$

**Step 5:** If possible, reduce the fraction to lowest terms. The fraction 9/4 can't be reduced.

**Step 6:** Change the improper fraction into a mixed number.

$$\begin{array}{r} 2 \\ 4\overline{)\,9} \\ 8 \\ \hline 1 \end{array}$$

Therefore, 1/4 × 9 = 2 1/4.

## Multiplying More Than Two Fractions

Any number of fractions can be multiplied. The procedure is basically the same as that used to multiply a pair of fractions.

**EXAMPLE:** ***Multiply 3/4 by 2/5 by 1/6.***

**Step 1:** Write the problem.

$$\frac{3}{4} \times \frac{2}{5} \times \frac{1}{6}$$

**Step 2:** Cancel, if possible.
The common number 2 divides into the numerator 2 and the denominator 4. Also, the common number 3 divides into the numerator 3 and the denominator 6.

$$\frac{\overset{1}{\cancel{3}}}{\underset{2}{\cancel{4}}} \times \frac{\overset{1}{\cancel{2}}}{5} \times \frac{1}{\underset{2}{\cancel{6}}}$$

**Step 3:** Multiply the numerators.

$$\frac{\overset{1}{\cancel{3}}}{\underset{2}{\cancel{4}}} \times \frac{\overset{1}{\cancel{2}}}{5} \times \frac{1}{\underset{2}{\cancel{6}}} = \frac{1}{\ }$$

**Step 4:** Multiply the denominators.

$$\frac{\overset{1}{\cancel{3}}}{\underset{2}{\cancel{4}}} \times \frac{\overset{1}{\cancel{2}}}{5} \times \frac{1}{\underset{2}{\cancel{6}}} = \frac{1}{20}$$

Therefore, 3/4 × 2/5 × 1/6 = 1/20.

## Multiplying Mixed Numbers

To multiply mixed numbers, first change the mixed numbers to improper fractions. After multiplying, change the improper fractions back to mixed numbers. If necessary, review chapter one to see how to change mixed numbers to improper fractions and vice versa.

**EXAMPLE: *Multiply 3⅙ by 2⅖.***

**Step 1:** Write the problem.

$$3\tfrac{1}{6} \times 2\tfrac{2}{5}$$

**Step 2:** Change the mixed numbers to improper fractions.

$$3\tfrac{1}{6} = \tfrac{19}{6}$$
$$2\tfrac{2}{5} = \tfrac{12}{5}$$

**Step 3:** Rewrite the problem.

$$\frac{19}{6} \times \frac{12}{5}$$

**Step 4:** Cancel, if possible.
The common number 6 divides into the numerator 12 and the denominator 6.

$$\frac{19}{\cancel{6}_1} \times \frac{\cancel{12}^2}{5}$$

**Step 5:** Multiply the numerators.

$$\frac{19}{\cancel{6}_1} \times \frac{\cancel{12}^2}{5} = \frac{38}{}$$

**Step 6:** Multiply the denominators.

$$\frac{19}{\cancel{6}_1} \times \frac{\cancel{12}^2}{5} = \frac{38}{5}$$

**Step 7:** Change the improper fraction to a mixed number.

$$5\overline{)38} = 7 \;\; \frac{35}{\phantom{0}3}$$

Therefore, $3\tfrac{1}{6} \times 2\tfrac{2}{5} = 7\tfrac{3}{5}$.

## Dividing Fractions

### Dividing a Fraction by a Fraction

The procedure for dividing one fraction by another is pretty straightforward. You simply invert the divisor (the number by which we divide) and then multiply the fractions. Let's look at an example.

**EXAMPLE: *Divide ¾ by ⅞.***

**Step 1:** Write the problem.

$$\frac{3}{4} \div \frac{7}{8}$$

The fraction ⅞ is the divisor, since it is the number by which we divide.

**Step 2:** Invert the divisor and change the operation from division to multiplication.

$$\frac{3}{4} \times \frac{8}{7}$$

**Step 3:** Cancel if possible.
The common number 4 divides into the numerator 8 and the denominator 4.

$$\frac{3}{\cancel{4}_{1}} \times \frac{\cancel{8}^{2}}{7}$$

**Step 4:** Multiply the numerators.

$$\frac{3}{\cancel{4}_{1}} \times \frac{\cancel{8}^{2}}{7} = \frac{6}{\phantom{7}}$$

**Step 5:** Multiply the denominators.

$$\frac{3}{\cancel{4}_{1}} \times \frac{\cancel{8}^{2}}{7} = \frac{6}{7}$$

Therefore, ¾ ÷ ⅞ = 6⁄7.

## Dividing a Whole Number by a Fraction

To divide a whole number by a fraction, first write the whole number as a fraction, then invert the divisor and multiply the fractions. Here's how it works.

**EXAMPLE:** *Divide 9 by ¾.*

**Step 1:** Write the problem, showing the whole number as a fraction.

$$\frac{9}{1} \div \frac{3}{4}$$

**Step 2:** Invert the divisor and change the operation from division to multiplication.

$$\frac{9}{1} \times \frac{4}{3}$$

**Step 3:** Cancel, if possible.
The common number 3 divides into the numerator 9 and the denominator 3.

$$\frac{\cancel{9}^{3}}{1} \times \frac{4}{\cancel{3}_{1}}$$

**Step 4:** Multiply the numerators.

$$\frac{\cancel{9}^{3}}{1} \times \frac{4}{\cancel{3}_{1}} = \frac{12}{\phantom{x}}$$

*Part One*

**BASIC WOODSHOP ARITHMETIC**

**Step 5:** Multiply the denominators.

$$\overset{3}{\underset{1}{\cancel{9}}} \times \frac{4}{\underset{1}{\cancel{3}}} = \frac{12}{1}$$

Therefore, converting to a whole number,
$9 \div \frac{3}{4} = 12$.

### Dividing Mixed Numbers

To divide mixed numbers, change the mixed numbers to improper fractions, then invert the divisor and multiply the fractions.

**EXAMPLE:** *Divide 3⅝ by 2¼.*

**Step 1:** Write the problem.

$$3\frac{5}{8} \div 2\frac{1}{4}$$

**Step 2:** Change the mixed numbers to improper fractions.

$$3\frac{5}{8} = \frac{29}{8}$$
$$2\frac{1}{4} = \frac{9}{4}$$

**Step 3:** Rewrite the problem.

$$\frac{29}{8} \div \frac{9}{4}$$

**Step 4:** Invert the divisor and change the operation from division to multiplication.

$$\frac{29}{8} \times \frac{4}{9}$$

**Step 5:** Cancel, if possible.
The common number 4 divides into the numerator 4 and the denominator 8.

$$\underset{2}{\cancel{8}} \times \frac{\overset{1}{\cancel{4}}}{9}$$ 
$$\frac{29}{\underset{2}{\cancel{8}}} \times \frac{\overset{1}{\cancel{4}}}{9}$$

**Step 6:** Multiply the numerators.

$$\frac{29}{\underset{2}{\cancel{8}}} \times \frac{\overset{1}{\cancel{4}}}{9} = \frac{29}{}$$

**Step 7:** Multiply the denominators.

$$\frac{29}{\underset{2}{\cancel{8}}} \times \frac{\overset{1}{\cancel{4}}}{9} = \frac{29}{18}$$

**Step 8:** Change the improper fraction to a mixed number.

$$\begin{array}{r} 1 \\ 18\overline{)29} \\ \underline{18} \\ 11 \end{array}$$

Therefore, $3\frac{5}{8} \div 2\frac{1}{4} = 1\frac{11}{18}$.

WOODSHOP APPLICATION

# *Working with Fractions*

You are building an Early American wall shelf that must measure 32⅞" in height (Fig. 2-1) to fit the available space. The four shelves, which each measure ¹³⁄₁₆" thick, are to be spaced 10⅝", 8⅜" and 6½" apart to accommodate your collection of hardcover and softcover books. From a visual standpoint, it's important for the space at the top and bottom of the wall shelf (dimension A) be the same. What is dimension A?

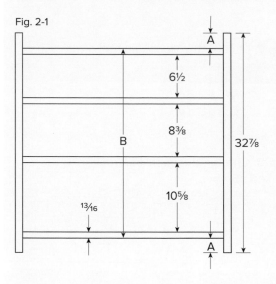

Fig. 2-1

To find A, determine the distance between the bottom shelf and the top shelf (dimension B), then subtract B from 32⅞" and divide the result by 2.

**Step 1:** Find the total thickness for all four shelves.

There are four shelves, each one ¹³⁄₁₆" thick, so multiply 4 by ¹³⁄₁₆ to find the total thickness for all four shelves.

First change the whole number 4 to a fraction (⁴⁄₁) and write the problem.

$$\frac{4}{1} \times \frac{13}{16} = \frac{52}{16}$$

Cancel.

$$\frac{\overset{1}{\cancel{4}}}{1} \times \frac{13}{\underset{4}{\cancel{16}}} = \frac{13}{4}$$

Change the improper fraction to a mixed number.

$$\begin{array}{r} 3 = 3¼ \\ 4\overline{)13} \\ \underline{12} \\ 1 \end{array}$$

Therefore, 4 × ¹³⁄₁₆" = 3¼.

**Step 2:** Find dimension B by adding the total thickness for all shelves (3¼) plus the distances between each of the shelves.

$$3¼ + 10⅝ + 8⅜ + 6½ =$$

Since this addition problem involves mixed numbers with unlike fractions, you'll need to find the lowest common denominator.

The lowest common denominator is 8.

Raise the fraction ¼ to higher terms with the common denominator 8, using 2 as the common number.

$$\frac{1 \times 2}{4 \times 2} = \frac{2}{8}$$

Raise the fraction ½ to higher terms with the common denominator 8, using 4 as the common number.

$$\frac{1 \times 4}{2 \times 4} = \frac{4}{8}$$

Rewrite the problem and add.

$$3\tfrac{2}{8} + 10\tfrac{5}{8} + 8\tfrac{3}{8} + 6\tfrac{4}{8} = 28\tfrac{6}{8} = 28\tfrac{3}{4}$$

Dimension B = 28¾".

**Step 3:** Subtract B from 32⅞".

$$32\tfrac{7}{8} - 28\tfrac{3}{4} =$$

Since the subtraction problem involves mixed numbers with unlike fractions, you'll need to find the lowest common denominator.

The lowest common denominator is 8.

Raise the fraction ¾ to higher terms with the common denominator 8, using 2 as the common number.

$$\frac{3 \times 2}{4 \times 2} = \frac{6}{8}$$

Rewrite the problem and subtract.

$$32\tfrac{7}{8} - 28\tfrac{6}{8} = 4\tfrac{1}{8}$$

Therefore, 32⅞" − 28¾" = 4⅛".

**Step 4:** Divide 4⅛ by 2.

$$4\tfrac{1}{8} \div 2$$

Convert the mixed number into an improper fraction and rewrite the problem.

$$4\tfrac{1}{8} = \tfrac{33}{8}$$
$$\tfrac{33}{8} \div 2$$

Write the problem with the whole number as a fraction.

$$\frac{33}{8} \div \frac{2}{1}$$

Invert the divisor and multiply.

$$\frac{33}{8} \times \frac{1}{2} = \frac{33}{16}$$

Change the improper fraction into a mixed number.

$$\begin{array}{r} 2 = 2\tfrac{1}{16} \\ 16\overline{)33} \\ \underline{32} \\ 1 \end{array}$$

Therefore, A = 2¹⁄₁₆".

CHAPTER 3

# *Understanding Decimals*

You know from chapter one that a fraction represents a part of a whole. But in our system of numbers, a fraction isn't the only way to show part of a whole. A *decimal* can also be used to show that a whole is made up of smaller parts. A decimal is simply a means of expressing a fraction that has a denominator of 10 or some multiple of 10. Fractions can be converted to decimals, and decimals can be converted to fractions.

Any positive number that can be expressed without a fraction or a decimal is called a *whole number.* A *mixed decimal* is a number consisting of a whole number and a decimal. A dot (.), called the *decimal point,* is used to separate the whole number from the decimal. Any number to the left of a decimal point is a whole number, while any number to the right of a decimal point is a decimal. For example, in the number 6.5, the number 6 is a whole number and the number .5 is a decimal. To look at it another way, any number to the left of the decimal point has a value of one or more, and any number to the right of the decimal point has a value of less than one.

A whole number is understood to have a decimal point at the end of the number, although the decimal point is not usually shown. We simply write 23, not 23., for example.

## Place Value and Decimals

Our system of arithmetic is based on the number ten. We create all of our numbers by collecting smaller numbers into groups of ten or multiples of ten. For example, the number 26 can be considered as two groups of ten plus a group of six ones.

$$26 = 2 \text{ tens} + 6 \text{ ones}$$
$$\text{or}$$
$$26 = 20 + 6$$

The number 598 can be considered as five groups of 100 (a multiple of ten) plus nine groups of ten plus a group of eight ones.

$$598 = 5 \text{ hundreds} + 9 \text{ tens} + 8 \text{ ones}$$
$$\text{or}$$
$$598 = 500 + 90 + 8$$

A number broken down into its component groups of ten or multiples of ten is said to be in *expanded form.*

The value of a digit depends upon its location, or place, in a number. The location of a digit in a number is called its *place value*. In the number 37, the digit 7 has a different place value than it does in the number 79. In the number 37, the digit 7 represents seven ones, or 7; in the number 79, the digit 7 represents seven tens, or 70.

## The Place Value Chart

Place value can best be shown using a chart. In the chart, each column heading represents a place value. Move one column to the left and place value is increased ten times. Move one column to the right and you have one-tenth the previous place value. For example, move one column to the left of the thousands place value and the value becomes ten thousand. But, move one column to the right of the thousands place value and you have a value of one hundred.

As mentioned earlier, the values to the right of the decimal point are less than one. The first column to the right of the decimal point represents tenths ($\frac{1}{10}$ or .1). Any number in that column has a value in tenths. Therefore, when considering the decimal .3, you know that its value is equal to three-tenths, or $\frac{3}{10}$, since the number 3 is in the tenths column. A decimal that extends to the tenths column is called a *one-place decimal*.

The column immediately to the right of the tenths column represents hundredths ($\frac{1}{100}$ or .01). So when considering the decimal .31, you know its value is equal to thirty-one hundredths, or $\frac{31}{100}$, since the number 31 extends to the hundredths column. A decimal that extends to the hundredths column is called a *two-place decimal*.

The column immediately to the right of the hundredths column represents thousandths ($\frac{1}{1000}$ or .001). When you see the decimal .547, you see that the number 547 extends to the thousandths column, so its value equals five hundred forty-seven thousandths, or $\frac{547}{1000}$. A decimal that extends to the thousandths column is called a *three-place decimal*.

Page space limits the number of place values shown, but no limit exists to the number of place values that can be used. Columns can be continually added to the left side of the decimal point to provide place values for numbers greater than one, like ten million, one hundred million, one billion, and so on. Also, columns can be added to the right side of the decimal point to provide place values for numbers less than one, like ten-millionths, hundred-millionths, billionths, etc. In woodworking, however, it's rare to work beyond the hundredths place when using decimals.

**PLACE VALUE CHART**

| Millions | Hundred Thousands | Ten Thousands | Thousands | Hundreds | Tens | Ones | **Decimal Point** | Tenths | Hundredths | Thousandths | Ten-Thousandths | Hundred-Thousandths | Millionths |
|---|---|---|---|---|---|---|---|---|---|---|---|---|---|

Let's use the place value chart to consider the whole number 30,624.

**PLACE VALUE CHART**

| Millions | Hundred Thousands | Ten Thousands | Thousands | Hundreds | Tens | Ones | Decimal Point | Tenths | Hundredths | Thousandths | Ten-Thousandths | Hundred-Thousandths | Millionths |
|---|---|---|---|---|---|---|---|---|---|---|---|---|---|
| | 3 | 0, | 6 | 2 | 4 | | | | | | | | |

Written in expanded form, the number 30,624 looks like this:

30,624 = 3 ten thousands + 0 thousands + 6 hundreds + 2 tens + 4 ones
or

| | | | |
|---|---|---|---|
| 3 ten thousands | = 3 x 10,000 | = 30,000 | |
| 0 thousands | = 0 x 1,000 | = 0,000 | |
| 6 hundreds | = 6 x 100 | = 600 | |
| 2 tens | = 2 x 10 | = 20 | |
| 4 ones | = 4 x 1 | = 4 | |
| TOTAL | | = 30,624 | |

Now, let's use the place value chart to look at the decimal number .476328.

**PLACE VALUE CHART**

| Millions | Hundred Thousands | Ten Thousands | Thousands | Hundreds | Tens | Ones | Decimal Point | Tenths | Hundredths | Thousandths | Ten-Thousandths | Hundred-Thousandths | Millionths |
|---|---|---|---|---|---|---|---|---|---|---|---|---|---|
| | | | | | | | . | 4 | 7 | 6 | 3 | 2 | 8 |

Written in expanded form, the number .476328 looks like this.
.476328 = 4 tenths + 7 hundredths + 6 thousandths + 3 ten-thousandths + 2 hundred-thousandths + 8 millionths
or

| | | | |
|---|---|---|---|
| 4 tenths | $= 4 \times \frac{1}{10}$ | $= 4 \times .1$ | = .4 |
| 7 hundredths | $= 7 \times \frac{1}{100}$ | $= 7 \times .01$ | = .07 |
| 6 thousandths | $= 6 \times \frac{1}{1000}$ | $= 6 \times .001$ | = .006 |
| 3 ten-thousandths | $= 3 \times \frac{1}{10,000}$ | $= 3 \times .0001$ | = .0003 |
| 2 hundred-thousandths | $= 2 \times \frac{1}{100,000}$ | $= 2 \times .00001$ | = .00002 |
| 8 millionths | $= 8 \times \frac{1}{1,000,000}$ | $= 8 \times .000001$ | = .000008 |
| TOTAL | | | = .476328 |

By the way, the decimal .476328 is read as *four hundred seventy-six thousand, three hundred twenty-eight millionths* or as *point four seven six three two eight.*

Let's look at a few other examples of decimal place values:

$.2 \quad = \frac{2}{10}$

$.7 \quad = \frac{7}{10}$

$.06 \quad = \frac{6}{100}$

$.37 \quad = \frac{37}{100}$

$.89 \quad = \frac{89}{100}$

$.009 = \frac{9}{1000}$

$.020 = \frac{20}{1000}$

$.104 \ = \frac{104}{1000}$

## Zero as a Placeholder

A zero (or zeros) located immediately to the right of the decimal point in a decimal number serve an important purpose. The zero keeps the number in its proper place. For example, to indicate three-thousandths, two zeros are placed between the decimal point and the number 3, resulting in the decimal .003. Without the two zeros, the decimal would be written .3, which we know is three-tenths, not three-thousandths.

## Adding Zero to the End of a Decimal

Adding a zero to the right of a decimal number does not change its value. Therefore, 6.5 = 6.50 = 6.500 = 6.5000 = 6.50000, and so on.

## Comparing Decimals

As you will recall from chapter one, it isn't always easy to quickly compare fractions. Let's say, for example, you want to know if $\frac{9}{16}$ is greater than $\frac{29}{64}$. To make the comparison, you need to find the common denominator. In this case it's 64. Then you must change $\frac{9}{16}$ to an equivalent fraction with 64 as the denominator, or $\frac{36}{64}$. Now, with both fractions having a common denominator, you can compare the fractions and see that $\frac{36}{64}$ ($\frac{9}{16}$) is greater than $\frac{29}{64}$.

Unlike fractions, it's relatively painless to compare the size of decimals because it's easy to find the common denominator. Let's look at a few examples.

**EXAMPLE 1:** *Is .3 greater than or less than .27?*

$$3 = .30 = \frac{30}{100}$$

$$.27 = \frac{27}{100}$$

Since $\frac{30}{100}$ is greater than $\frac{27}{100}$, .3 is greater than .27.

**EXAMPLE 2:** *Is .64 greater than or less than .083?*

$$.64 = .640 = \frac{640}{1000}$$

$$.083 = \frac{83}{1000}$$

Since $\frac{640}{1000}$ is greater than $\frac{83}{1000}$, .64 is greater than .83.

**EXAMPLE 3:** *Is .009 greater than or less than .0156?*

$$.009 = .0090 = \frac{90}{10,000}$$

$$.0156 = \frac{156}{10,000}$$

Since $\frac{90}{10,000}$ is less than $\frac{156}{10,000}$, .009 is less than .0156.

## Changing a Decimal to a Fraction

To change a decimal into a fraction:

**Step 1:** Produce the numerator by writing the decimal number without the decimal point and without any placeholders.

**Step 2:** Produce the denominator by writing the appropriate number (which will be 10 or some multiple of 10) based on the place value of the decimal.

**Step 3:** If possible, reduce the fraction to lowest terms. Let's look at a few examples.

**EXAMPLE 1:** *Change .8 to a fraction.*

**Step 1:** Remove the decimal point and write the decimal number.

$$\underline{8}$$

**Step 2:** Since the decimal of .8 is in the tenths place value, the denominator is 10.

$$\frac{8}{10}$$

**Step 3:** In this case, the fraction can be reduced.

$$\frac{8 \div 2}{10 \div 2} = \frac{4}{5}$$

Therefore, the decimal .8 equals the fraction $\frac{8}{10}$ or $\frac{4}{5}$.

**EXAMPLE 2:** *Change .27 to a fraction.*

**Step 1:** Remove the decimal point and write the decimal number.

$$\underline{27}$$

**Step 2:** Since the decimal of .27 is in the hundredths place value, the denominator is 100.

$$\frac{27}{100}$$

**Step 3:** In this case, the fraction can't be reduced.

Therefore, the decimal .27 equals the fraction $\frac{27}{100}$.

**EXAMPLE 3:** *Change .375 to a fraction.*

**Step 1:** Remove the decimal point and write the decimal number.

$$.375$$

**Step 2:** Since the decimal of .375 is in the thousandths place value, the denominator is 1000.

$$\frac{375}{1000}$$

**Step 3:** In this case, the fraction can be reduced.

$$\frac{375 \div 125}{1000 \div 125} = \frac{3}{8}$$

Therefore, the decimal .375 equals the fraction $^{375}/_{1000}$, or ⅜.

## Changing a Fraction to a Decimal

To change a fraction to a decimal, divide the numerator by the denominator. Chapter four explains this type of division.

CHAPTER 4

# Working with Decimals

Decimals, like fractions, can be added, subtracted, multiplied and divided. This chapter shows how to perform these operations.

## Adding Decimals

The procedure for adding decimals is straightforward. First, you write the numbers in column form with the decimal points aligned vertically, then you add the numbers in the same way that whole numbers are added. A decimal point is placed in the total so it aligns with the decimal points in the numbers you are adding. Here are a couple of examples.

**EXAMPLE 1:** *Add .25 and .31.*

**Step 1:** Write the numbers in column form with the decimal points aligned vertically.

$$
\begin{array}{r}
.25 \\
+\,.31 \\
\hline
\end{array}
$$

**Step 2:** Add the numbers.

$$
\begin{array}{r}
.25 \\
+\,.31 \\
\hline
56
\end{array}
$$

**Step 3:** Place the decimal point in the total so it aligns vertically with the other decimal points.

$$
\begin{array}{r}
.25 \\
+\,.31 \\
\hline
.56
\end{array}
$$

**EXAMPLE 2:** *Add .324, 251 and .124.*

**Step 1:** Write the numbers in column form with the decimal points aligned vertically.

$$
\begin{array}{r}
.324 \\
.251 \\
+\,.124 \\
\hline
\end{array}
$$

**Step 2:** Add the numbers.

$$
\begin{array}{r}
.324 \\
.251 \\
+\,.124 \\
\hline
699
\end{array}
$$

**Step 3:** Place the decimal point in the total so it aligns vertically with the other decimal points.

```
  .324
  .251
+ .124
 ─────
  .699
```

## Adding Mixed Decimals

You will recall from chapter three that a mixed decimal is a number consisting of a whole number and a decimal. Let's look at a couple of examples to see how to add them.

**EXAMPLE 1:** *Add 12.38 and 5.76.*

**Step 1:** Write the numbers in column form with the decimal points aligned vertically.

```
  12.38
+  5.76
 ──────
```

**Step 2:** Add the numbers.

```
  12.38
+  5.76
 ──────
  18 14
```

**Step 3:** Place the decimal point in the total so it aligns vertically with the other decimal points.

```
  12.38
+  5.76
 ──────
  18.14
```

**EXAMPLE 2:** *Add 7.29 and .48.*

**Step 1:** Write the numbers in column form with the decimal points aligned vertically.

```
  7.29
+  .48
 ─────
```

**Step 2:** Add the numbers.

```
  7.29
+  .48
 ─────
  7 77
```

**Step 3:** Place the decimal point in the total so it aligns vertically with the other decimal points.

```
  7.29
+  .48
 ─────
  7.77
```

## Adding When the Decimal Has Zeros

From chapter three, you will recall that a zero to the left of a decimal number serves as an important placeholder for the number.

**EXAMPLE 1:** *Add .05 and .22.*

**Step 1:** Write the numbers in column form with the decimal points aligned vertically.

```
  .05
+ .22
 ────
```

**Step 2:** Add the numbers.

```
  .05
+ .22
 ────
  27
```

**Step 3:** Place the decimal point in the total so it aligns vertically with the other decimal points.

$$
\begin{array}{r}
.05 \\
+\ .22 \\
\hline
.27
\end{array}
$$

**EXAMPLE 2:** *Add .007 and .305.*

**Step 1:** Write the numbers in column form with the decimal points aligned vertically.

$$
\begin{array}{r}
.007 \\
+\ .305 \\
\hline
\end{array}
$$

**Step 2:** Add the numbers.

$$
\begin{array}{r}
.007 \\
+\ .305 \\
\hline
312
\end{array}
$$

**Step 3:** Place the decimal point in the total so it aligns vertically with the other decimal points.

$$
\begin{array}{r}
.007 \\
+\ .305 \\
\hline
.312
\end{array}
$$

Also from chapter three, remember that adding a zero to the right of a decimal does not change its value.

**EXAMPLE 3:** *Add .75 and .384.*

**Step 1:** Write the numbers in column form with the decimal points aligned vertically.

$$
\begin{array}{r}
.75 \\
+\ .384 \\
\hline
\end{array}
$$

**Step 2:** Since .384 is a three-place decimal, convert .75 into a three-place decimal by adding a zero. (This step is optional since a zero is understood to exist.)

$$
\begin{array}{r}
.750 \\
+\ .384 \\
\hline
\end{array}
$$

**Step 3:** Add the numbers.

$$
\begin{array}{r}
.750 \\
+\ .384 \\
\hline
1\ 134
\end{array}
$$

**Step 4:** Place the decimal point in the total so it aligns vertically with the other decimal points.

$$
\begin{array}{r}
.750 \\
+\ .384 \\
\hline
1.134
\end{array}
$$

Note in this example the addition of two decimal fractions results in a mixed decimal.

**EXAMPLE 4:** *Add .005, .5026 and .3.*

**Step 1:** Write the numbers in column form with the decimal points aligned vertically.

$$
\begin{array}{r}
.005 \\
.5026 \\
+\ .3 \\
\hline
\end{array}
$$

**Step 2:** Since .5026 is a four-place decimal, change .005 and .3 into four-place decimals by adding zeros as needed.

$$
\begin{array}{r}
.0050 \\
.5026 \\
+\ .3000 \\
\hline
\end{array}
$$

**Step 3:** Add the numbers.

```
  .0050
  .5026
+ .3000
  8076
```

**Step 4:** Place the decimal point in the total so it aligns vertically with the other decimal points.

```
  .0050
  .5026
+ .3000
  .8076
```

## Subtracting Decimals

Decimal numbers are subtracted much like whole numbers are subtracted. First you write the numbers in column form, keeping the decimal points aligned vertically, then you subtract the numbers to produce a difference. The decimal point is placed in the difference so it aligns vertically with decimal points in the numbers you are subtracting.

**EXAMPLE 1:** *Subtract .43 from .76.*

**Step 1:** Write the numbers in column form with the decimal points aligned vertically.

```
  .76
− .43
```

**Step 2:**  Subtract the numbers.

```
  .76
− .43
  33
```

**Step 3:** Add the numbers.

```
  .76
− .43
  .33
```

**EXAMPLE 2:** *Subtract .648 from .765.*

**Step 1:** Write the numbers in column form with the decimal points aligned vertically.

```
  .765
− .648
```

**Step 2:** Subtract the numbers.

```
  .765
− .648
  117
```

**Step 3:** Place the decimal point in the difference so it aligns vertically with the other decimal points.

```
  .765
− .648
  .117
```

## Subtracting Mixed Decimals

A mixed decimal is subtracted in the same manner as a decimal number is subtracted.

**EXAMPLE 1:** *Subtract 128.697 from 483.953.*

**Step 1:** Write the numbers in column form with the decimal points aligned vertically.

```
  483.953
− 128.697
```

**Step 2:** Subtract the numbers.

$$
\begin{array}{r}
483.953 \\
-128.697 \\
\hline
355\ 256
\end{array}
$$

**Step 3:** Place the decimal point in the difference so it aligns vertically with the other decimal points.

$$
\begin{array}{r}
483.953 \\
-128.697 \\
\hline
355.256
\end{array}
$$

**EXAMPLE 2:** *Subtract .28 from 7.15.*

**Step 1:** Write the numbers in column form with the decimal points aligned vertically.

$$
\begin{array}{r}
7.15 \\
-.28 \\
\hline
\end{array}
$$

**Step 2:** Subtract the numbers.

$$
\begin{array}{r}
7.15 \\
-.28 \\
\hline
6\ 87
\end{array}
$$

**Step 3:** Place the decimal point in the difference so it aligns vertically with the other decimal points.

$$
\begin{array}{r}
7.15 \\
-.28 \\
\hline
6.87
\end{array}
$$

## Subtracting When the Decimal Has Zeros as Placeholders

A zero between the decimal point and a decimal number serves to keep the number in its proper place value.

**EXAMPLE 1:** *Subtract .08 from .59.*

**Step 1:** Write the numbers in column form with the decimal points aligned vertically.

$$
\begin{array}{r}
.59 \\
-.08 \\
\hline
\end{array}
$$

**Step 2:** Subtract the numbers.

$$
\begin{array}{r}
.59 \\
-.08 \\
\hline
51
\end{array}
$$

**Step 3:** Place the decimal point in the difference so it aligns vertically with the other decimal points.

$$
\begin{array}{r}
.59 \\
-.08 \\
\hline
.51
\end{array}
$$

**EXAMPLE 2:** *Subtract .005 from .602.*

**Step 1:** Write the numbers in column form with the decimal points aligned vertically.

$$
\begin{array}{r}
.602 \\
-.005 \\
\hline
\end{array}
$$

**Step 2:** Subtract the numbers.

```
  .602
− .005
  597
```

**Step 3:** Place the decimal point in the difference so it aligns vertically with the other decimal points.

```
  .602
− .005
  .597
```

**EXAMPLE 3:** *Subtract .4 from .756.*

**Step 1:** Write the numbers in column form with the decimal points aligned vertically.

```
  .756
− .4
```

**Step 2:** Since .756 is a three-place decimal, make .4 a three-place decimal by adding two zeros. (This step is optional, since the zeros are understood to exist.)

```
  .756
− .400
```

**Step 3:** Subtract the numbers.

```
  .756
− .400
  356
```

**Step 4:** Place the decimal point in the difference so it aligns vertically with the other decimal points.

```
  .756
− .400
  .356
```

**EXAMPLE 4:** *Subtract .69243 from .95.*

**Step 1:** Write the numbers in column form with the decimal points aligned vertically.

```
  .95
− .69243
```

**Step 2:** Since .69243 is a five-place decimal, change .95 into a five-place decimal by adding zeros.

```
  .95000
− .69243
```

**Step 3:** Subtract the numbers.

```
  .95000
− .69243
  25757
```

**Step 4:** Place the decimal point in the difference so it aligns vertically with the other decimal points.

```
  .95000
− .69243
  .25757
```

## Multiplying Decimals

Decimal numbers are multiplied in the same manner as whole numbers. Unlike adding or subtracting decimals, there is no need to vertically align the decimal points of the numbers being multiplied. Keep in mind that the number of decimal places in the product must equal the total number of decimal places in the numbers being multiplied. Here are some examples.

**EXAMPLE 1:** *Multiply .34 by .7.*

**Step 1:** Write the numbers.

$$
\begin{array}{r}
.34 \\
\times\ .7 \\
\end{array}
$$

**Step 2:** Multiply the numbers as you would whole numbers.

$$
\begin{array}{r}
.34 \\
\times\ .7 \\
\hline
238 \\
\end{array}
$$

**Step 3:** Place the decimal point in the product. Since .34 is a two-place decimal and .7 is a one-place decimal, the total number of decimal places in the numbers being multiplied is three. Therefore, the number of decimal places in the product must equal three. Counting three decimal places from right to left, the product becomes .238.

$$
\begin{array}{r}
.34 \\
\times\ .7 \\
\hline
.238 \\
\end{array}
$$

**EXAMPLE 2:** *Multiply .632 by .85.*

**Step 1.** Write the numbers.

$$
\begin{array}{r}
.632 \\
\times\ .85 \\
\end{array}
$$

**Step 2:** Multiply the numbers as you would whole numbers.

$$
\begin{array}{r}
.632 \\
\times\ \ .85 \\
\hline
3160 \\
5056\ \ \\
\hline
53720 \\
\end{array}
$$

**Step 3:** Place the decimal point in the product. Since .632 is a three-place decimal and .85 is a two-place decimal, the total number of decimal places in the numbers being multiplied is five. Therefore, the number of decimal places in the product must equal five. Counting five decimal places from right to left, the product becomes .53720.

$$
\begin{array}{r}
.632 \\
\times\ \ .85 \\
\hline
3160 \\
5056\ \ \\
\hline
.53720 \\
\end{array}
$$

**EXAMPLE 3:** *Multiply .08 by .5.*

**Step 1:** Write the numbers.

$$
\begin{array}{r}
.08 \\
\times\ .5 \\
\end{array}
$$

BASIC WOODSHOP ARITHMETIC

Part One

**Step 2:** Multiply the numbers as you would whole numbers.

```
    .08
 ×  .5
   ‾‾‾
    40
```

**Step 3:** Place the decimal point in the product.

   Since .08 is a two-place decimal and .5 is a one-place decimal, the total number of decimal places in the numbers being multiplied is three. Therefore, the number of decimal places in the product must equal three. Counting three decimal places from right to left, the product becomes .040. Note that a zero must be inserted to create a three-place decimal.

```
    .08
 ×  .5
   ‾‾‾
  .040
```

**EXAMPLE 4:** *Multiply .00785 by .25.*

**Step 1:** Write the numbers.

```
  .00785
 ×   .25
  ‾‾‾‾‾‾
```

**Step 2:** Multiply the numbers as you would whole numbers.

```
  .00785
 ×   .25
  ‾‾‾‾‾‾
   3925
  1570
  ‾‾‾‾‾
  19625
```

**Step 3:** Place the decimal point in the product.

   Since .00785 is a five-place decimal and .25 is a two-place decimal, the total number of decimal places in the numbers being multiplied is seven. Therefore, the number of decimal places in the product must equal seven. Counting seven decimal places from right to left, the product becomes .0019625. Note that two zeros must be inserted to create a seven-place decimal.

```
   .00785
 ×    .25
  ‾‾‾‾‾‾‾
    3925
   1570
  ‾‾‾‾‾‾‾
 .0019625
```

## Multiplying Mixed Decimals

Mixed decimals are multiplied in the same manner as decimal numbers.

**EXAMPLE 1:** *Multiply 4.65 by .75.*

**Step 1:** Write the numbers.

```
   4.65
 ×  .75
  ‾‾‾‾‾
```

**Step 2:** Multiply the numbers as you would whole numbers.

```
   4.65
 ×  .75
  ‾‾‾‾‾
   2325
  3255
  ‾‾‾‾‾
  34875
```

**Step 3:** Place the decimal point in the product.

Since 4.65 has a two-place decimal and .75 is a two-place decimal, the total number of decimal places in the numbers being multiplied is four. Therefore, the number of decimal places in the product must equal four. Counting four decimal places from right to left, the product becomes 3.4875.

$$
\begin{array}{r}
4.65 \\
\times\ .75 \\
\hline
2325 \\
3255\ \ \\
\hline
3.4875
\end{array}
$$

***Example 2: Multiply 15.375 by 6.75.***

**Step 1:** Write the numbers.

$$
\begin{array}{r}
15.375 \\
\times\ \ 6.75 \\
\hline
\end{array}
$$

**Step 2:** Multiply the numbers as you would whole numbers.

$$
\begin{array}{r}
15.375 \\
\times\ \ \ \ 6.75 \\
\hline
76875 \\
107625\ \ \\
92250\ \ \ \\
\hline
10378125
\end{array}
$$

**Step 3:** Place the decimal point in the product.

Since 15.375 has a three-place decimal and 6.75 has a two-place decimal, the total number of decimal places in the numbers being multiplied is five. Therefore, the number of decimal places in the product must equal five. Counting five decimal places from right to left, the product becomes 103.78125.

$$
\begin{array}{r}
15.375 \\
\times\ \ \ \ \ 6.75 \\
\hline
76875 \\
107625\ \ \\
92250\ \ \ \\
\hline
103.78125
\end{array}
$$

## Dividing Decimals

Decimal numbers are divided in the same way that whole numbers are divided.

To determine the correct location of the decimal point in the quotient, move the divisor decimal point to the right as many places as are needed to make the divisor a whole number, then move the dividend decimal point to the right the same number of places. Place the decimal point in the quotient directly above the new location of the dividend decimal point. Here are some examples.

**EXAMPLE 1:** *Divide .15 by .3.*

**Step 1:** Write the problem.

$$.3\overline{).15}$$

**Step 2:** Move the divisor decimal point to the right as many places as are needed to make a whole number. To make the divisor (.3) a whole number, move the decimal one place to the right. The result is the whole number 3.

$$3.\overline{).15}$$

**Step 3:** Move the dividend decimal point to the right the same number of places that you moved the divisor decimal point. Since the divisor decimal point was moved one place to the right, you must move the dividend (.15) decimal point one place to the right. The result is the number 1.5.

$$3.\overline{)1.5}$$

**Step 4:** Place the decimal point in the quotient.

$$3.\overline{)1.5}$$

**Step 5:** Divide the numbers.

$$
\begin{array}{r}
.5 \\
3.\overline{)1.5} \\
\underline{15} \\
0
\end{array}
$$

Therefore, .15 ÷ .3 = .5.

**EXAMPLE 2:** *Divide .75 by .25.*

**Step 1:** Write the problem.

$$.25\overline{).75}$$

**Step 2:** Move the divisor decimal point to the right as many places as are needed to make the divisor a whole number. To make the divisor (.25) a whole number, move the decimal two places to the right. The result is the whole number 25.

$$25.\overline{).75}$$

**Step 3:** Move the dividend decimal point to the right the same number of places that you moved the divisor decimal point. Since the divisor decimal point was moved two places to the right, you must move the dividend (.75) decimal point two places to the right. The result is the number 75.

$$25.\overline{)75.}$$

**Step 4:** Place the decimal point in the quotient.

$$25.\overline{)75.}$$

**Step 5:** Divide the numbers.

$$
\begin{array}{r}
3 \\
25.\overline{)75.} \\
\underline{75} \\
0
\end{array}
$$

Therefore, .75 ÷ .25 = 3.

**EXAMPLE 3:** *Divide .64 by .004.*

**Step 1:** Write the problem.

$$.004\overline{).64}$$

**Step 2:** Move the divisor decimal point to the right as many places as are needed to make the divisor a whole number. To make the divisor (.004) a whole number, move the decimal three places to the right. The result is the whole number 4.

$$4.\overline{).64}$$

**Step 3:** Move the dividend decimal point to the right the same number of places that you moved the divisor decimal point.

 Since the divisor decimal point was moved three places to the right, you must move the dividend (.64) decimal point three places to the right. The result is the number 640. Note that it is necessary to add a zero in order to move the decimal three places.

$$4.\overline{)640.}$$

**Step 4:** Place the decimal point in the quotient.

$$4.\overline{)640.}$$

**Step 5:** Divide the numbers.

```
      160.
4.)640.
    4
    24
    24
     0
```

Therefore, .64 ÷ .004 = 160

## When Decimals Won't Divide Evenly

Not all decimals divide evenly. When division results in a quotient and a remainder, simply round off the quotient to an acceptable place value. Here is an example.

**EXAMPLE 1:** *Divide .38 by .6.*

**Step 1:** Write the problem.

$$.6\overline{).38}$$

**Step 2:** Move the divisor decimal point to the right as many places as are needed to make the divisor a whole number. To make the divisor (.6) a whole number, move the decimal one place to the right. The result is the whole number 6.

$$6.\overline{).38}$$

**Step 3:** Move the dividend decimal point to the right the same number of places that you moved the divisor decimal point. Since the divisor decimal point was moved one place to the right, you must move the dividend (.38) decimal point one place to the right. The result is the number 3.8.

$$6.\overline{)3.8}$$

**Step 4:** Place the decimal point in the quotient.

$$6.\overline{)3.8}$$

**Step 5:** Divide the numbers.

```
      .63333
6.)3.80000
   3 6
    20
    18
     20
     18
      20
      18
       2
```

Since the number does not divide evenly, round the number to an acceptable value. A two-place decimal is acceptable for most woodworking, so the number becomes .63. Therefore, .38 + .6 = .63.

## Dividing Mixed Decimals

A mixed decimal is divided in the same manner as a decimal fraction is divided.

**EXAMPLE 1:** *Divide 3.5 by .875.*

**Step 1:** Write the problem.

$$.875\overline{)3.5}$$

**Step 2:** Move the divisor decimal point to the right as many places as are needed to make the divisor a whole number. To make the divisor (.875) a whole number, move the decimal three places to the right. The result is the whole number 875.

$$875.\overline{)3.5}$$

**Step 3:** Move the dividend decimal point to the right the same number of places that you moved the divisor decimal point. Since the divisor decimal point was moved three places to the right, you must move the dividend (3.5) decimal point three places to the right. The result is the number 3500. Note that it is necessary to add two zeros in order to move the decimal three places.

$$875.\overline{)3500.}$$

**Step 4:** Place the decimal point in the quotient.

$$875.\overline{)3500.}^{\,\cdot}$$

**Step 5:** Divide the numbers.

```
           4.
875.)3500.
     3500
        0
```

Therefore, 3.5 ÷ .875 = 4.

**EXAMPLE 2:** *Divide .24 by 6.*

**Step 1:** Write the problem.

$$6\overline{)\,.24}$$

**Step 2:** Move the divisor decimal point to the right as many places as are needed to make the divisor a whole number.

Since the divisor already is a whole number, there is no need to move the decimal point.

*Part One*

**BASIC WOODSHOP ARITHMETIC**

**Step 3:** Move the dividend decimal point to the right the same number of places that you moved the divisor decimal point.

Since the divisor decimal point was not moved, you don't need to move the dividend decimal point.

**Step 4:** Place the decimal point in the quotient.

$$6\overline{).24}$$

**Step 5:** Divide the numbers.

$$\begin{array}{r} .04 \\ 6\overline{).24} \\ \underline{24} \\ 0 \end{array}$$

Therefore, .24 ÷ 6 = .04. Note that a zero was used in the quotient as a placeholder.

**EXAMPLE 3: *Divide 194.6875 by 22.25.***

**Step 1:** Write the problem.

$$22.25\overline{)194.6875}$$

**Step 2:** Move the divisor decimal point to the right as many places as are needed to make the divisor a whole number. To make the divisor (22.25) a whole number, move the decimal two places to the right. The result is the whole number 2225.

$$2225.\overline{)194.6875}$$

**Step 3:** Move the dividend decimal point to the right the same number of places that you moved the divisor decimal point. Since the divisor decimal point was moved two places to the right, you must move the dividend (194.6875) decimal point two places to the right. The result is the number 19468.75.

$$2225.\overline{)19468.75}$$

**Step 4:** Place the decimal point in the quotient.

$$2225.\overline{)19468.75}$$

**Step 5:** Divide the numbers.

$$\begin{array}{r} 8.75 \\ 2225.\overline{)19468.75} \\ 17800 \\ 16687 \\ 15575 \\ 11125 \\ 11125 \\ 0 \end{array}$$

Therefore, 194.6875 ÷ 22.25 = 8.75.

## Changing a Fraction to a Decimal

Changing a fraction into a decimal is easy: You simply divide the numerator of the fraction by the denominator. (To see how to change a decimal into a fraction, refer to chapter three.)

**EXAMPLE 1: *Change ¼ into a decimal.***

**Step 1:** Write the problem, dividing the numerator by the denominator.

$$4\overline{)1}$$

**Step 2:** Add a decimal point after the numerator (the dividend).

$$4\overline{)1.}$$

**Step 3:** Add zeros as needed. (You can add more zeros as you divide the numbers, if necessary).

$$4\overline{)1.00}$$

**Step 4:** Place the decimal point in the quotient.

$$4\overline{)1.00}^{\ \ .}$$

**Step 5:** Divide the numbers.

```
      .25
 4)1.00
   8
   20
   20
    0
```

Therefore, ¼ = .25.

**EXAMPLE 2:** *Change ²³/₃₂ into a decimal.*

**Step 1:** Write the problem, dividing the numerator by the denominator.

$$32\overline{)23}$$

**Step 2:** Add a decimal point after the numerator (the dividend).

$$32\overline{)23.}$$

**Step 3:** Add zeros as needed.

$$32\overline{)23.00000}$$

**Step 4:** Place the decimal point in the quotient.

$$32\overline{)23.00000}^{\ \ \ .}$$

**Step 5:** Divide the numbers.

```
       .71875
 32)23.00000
    22 4
       60
       32
      280
      256
       240
       224
        160
        160
          0
```

Therefore, ²³/₃₂, = .71875, or .72 (rounded off to two decimal places).

**WOODSHOP APPLICATION**

## *Working with Decimals*

A chart shows that 1x10 lumber contains .84 board feet of lumber for each linear foot. If you need 65 board feet of 1x10 lumber for a project, how many linear feet of the lumber must you buy?

Divide 65 board feet by .84 to find out how many linear feet of 1x10 lumber are needed.

$$.84\overline{)65}$$

Move the decimal points and divide.

```
         77.38
84.)6500.00
    588
     620
     588
     320
     252
     680
     672
       8
```

You'll need about 77½ linear feet of 1x10 lumber to yield 65 board feet.

CHAPTER 5

# *Powers and Roots*

Some woodworkers might say an understanding of powers and roots is of little practical value in the woodshop. I suspect, however, that such skeptics would be surprised to learn that squares, square roots, cube roots and the like are often encountered when sawdust is flying. Indeed, a number of the formulas found in chapter seven (Plane Figure Formulas), chapter eight (Solid Figure Formulas) and chapter fourteen (Applying Handy Workshop Formulas) incorporate the principles of powers and roots. A table of powers and roots for fractions from $\frac{1}{64}$ to $\frac{63}{64}$ and whole numbers from 1 to 100 can be found in the appendix.

## Understanding Powers

Numbers multiplied together to form a product are called factors. For example, in the equation $2 \times 4 = 8$, the factors are 2 and 4. In $5 \times 1 \times 3 = 15$, the factors are 5, 1 and 3.

In arithmetic, a factor is sometimes repeatedly multiplied; for example, $3 \times 3$, or $7 \times 7 \times 7$ or $14 \times 14 \times 14 \times 14$. When a factor is repeatedly multiplied, the product that results is called a *power*. Therefore, 9 is a power of $3 \times 3$ (since $3 \times 3 = 9$), 343 is a power of $7 \times 7 \times 7$ (since $7 \times 7 \times 7 = 343$) and 38,416 is a power of $14 \times 14 \times 14 \times 14$ (since $14 \times 14 \times 14 \times 14 = 38,416$).

The factor that is repeatedly multiplied is called the base. The above examples have bases of 3, 7 and 14, respectively.

## Exponents

Repeatedly writing the base number to show repeated multiplication can get cumbersome. For example, to multiply the factor 2 by itself eight times you must write $2 \times 2 \times 2 \times 2 \times 2 \times 2 \times 2 \times 2$. In order to avoid having to write such long chains of numbers, we instead use a form of shorthand called an *exponent*. An exponent, which is written in a small raised (superscript) number adjacent to the base number, represents the number of times a base number must be repeatedly multiplied. Therefore, to show that the factor 2 is to be multiplied by itself eight times, you simply write $2^8$. This is read as *2 to the eighth power*. Here are a few other examples of exponents.

**EXAMPLE 1:** *Find the value of $9^4$.*

$$9^4 = 9 \times 9 \times 9 \times 9 = 6561$$

Note that for 9 to the fourth power, the base is 9, the exponent is 4 and the power is 6561.

**EXAMPLE 2:** *Find the value of $5^5$.*

$$5^5 = 5 \times 5 \times 5 \times 5 \times 5 = 3125.$$

Note that for 5 to the fifth power, the base is 5, the exponent is 5 and the power is 3125.

**EXAMPLE 3: *What is the sixth power of 3?***

$$3^6 = 3 \times 3 \times 3 \times 3 \times 3 \times 3 = 729$$

For 3 to the sixth power, the base is 3, the exponent is 6 and the power is 729.

**EXAMPLE 4: *What is the value of $4^2$?***

$$4^2 = 4 \times 4 = 16$$

The base is 4, the exponent is 2 and the power is 16. This can be read as *4 to the second power,* but the exponent 2 is commonly read as *squared.* Therefore, $4^2$ is read as *4 squared.*

**EXAMPLE 5: *What is the value of $7^3$?***

$$7^3 = 7 \times 7 \times 7 = 343$$

The base is 7, the exponent is 3 and the power is 343. This can be read as *7 to the third power,* but the exponent 3 is generally read as *cubed.* Therefore, $7^3$ is read as *7 cubed.*

## Exponents When the Base Is a Fraction

When using exponents, the base number is not always going to be a whole number. It can sometimes be a fraction. Before you start fretting that a mix of exponents and fractions is sure to trigger a math-induced headache, you'll be relieved to know that the procedure is actually straightforward. Indeed, the procedure is much the same as the one used in chapter two to multiply fractions.

Keep in mind that when the base number is a fraction, it can be either a proper fraction or an improper fraction. The power of a proper fraction always has less than the base number.

Conversely, the power of an improper fraction always has greater value than the base number. Let's look at some examples.

**EXAMPLE 1: *Find the value of $(\frac{2}{3})^2$.***

$$\frac{2}{3}^2 = \frac{2^2}{3^2} = \frac{2 \times 2}{3 \times 3} = \frac{4}{9}$$

**EXAMPLE 2: *What is $(\frac{3}{4})^4$?***

$$\frac{3}{4}^4 = \frac{3^4}{4^4} = \frac{3 \times 3 \times 3 \times 3}{4 \times 4 \times 4 \times 4} = \frac{81}{256}$$

**EXAMPLE 3: *Find the value of $(\frac{5}{2})^3$.***

$$\frac{5}{2}^3 = \frac{5^3}{2^3} = \frac{5 \times 5 \times 5}{2 \times 2 \times 2} = \frac{125}{8}$$

If desired, the improper fraction $\frac{125}{8}$ can be converted to the mixed fraction $15\frac{5}{8}$.

## Exponents When the Base Is a Decimal Number

Not only can a base number be a whole number or a fraction, it can also be a decimal number. When the base is a decimal number, the procedure is much the same as the one used to multiply decimals in chapter four. To raise a decimal number to a power, you simply multiply the decimal number by itself as many times as indicated by the exponent. Here are some examples.

**EXAMPLE 1: *What is the value of .25³?***

$$.25^3 = .25 \times .25 \times .25 = .015625$$

**EXAMPLE 2: *Find the value of .5².***

$$.5^2 = .5 \times .5 = .25$$

**EXAMPLE 3: *What is the value of .375⁵?***

$$.375^5 = .375 \times .375 \times .375 \times .375 \times .375 = .0074157$$

**EXAMPLE 4: *What is the value of 4.27²?***

$$4.27^2 = 4.27 \times 4.27 = 18.2329$$

## Determining the Power of a Power

You might, on occasion, come across a formula that requires you to find the power of a power. Let's work through some examples to show you how it's done.

**EXAMPLE 1: *Find the value of (4²)³.***

$$(4^2)^3 = (4 \times 4)^3$$
$$= 16^3$$
$$= 16 \times 16 \times 16$$
$$= 4096$$

## Optional Method

You can also find the value by first multiplying the two exponents to determine the new exponent. Then, using the new exponent, raise the base number to its power. Here's how it works.

$$(4^2)^3 = 4^{2 \times 3} = 4^6$$
$$= 4 \times 4 \times 4 \times 4 \times 4 \times 4$$
$$= 4096$$

**EXAMPLE 2: *Find the value of (2.5²)².***

$$(2.5^2)^2 = (2.5 \times 2.5)^2$$
$$= (6.25)^2$$
$$= 6.25 \times 6.25$$
$$= 39.0625$$

## Optional Method
$$(2.5^2)^2 = 2.5^{2 \times 2} = 2.5^4$$
$$= 2.5 \times 2.5 \times 2.5 \times 2.5$$
$$= 39.0625$$

## Multiplying Like Bases: A Shortcut

When two or more like bases are to be multiplied, you can use this shortcut to save time and effort. Simply add the exponents to determine a new exponent. Then, using the new exponent, raise the common base number to its power. Here's how to do it. (Remember, this shortcut can be used only when you have like bases.)

**EXAMPLE 1: *Multiply 5² by 5³.***

$$5^2 \times 5^3 = 5^{2 + 3}$$
$$= 5^5$$
$$= 5 \times 5 \times 5 \times 5 \times 5$$
$$= 3125$$

**EXAMPLE 2:** *Multiply $3^2$ by $3^2$ by $3^3$.*

$$3^2 \times 3^2 \times 3^3 = 3^{2+2+3}$$
$$= 3^7$$
$$= 3 \times 3 \times 3 \times 3 \times 3 \times 3 \times 3$$
$$= 2187$$

**EXAMPLE 3:** *Multiply $7^4 \times 3^2$.*
Since the bases are unlike numbers (7 and 3), you can't use the shortcut. Instead, you must determine each power, then do the multiplication.

$$7^4 \times 3^2 = (7 \times 7 \times 7 \times 7) \times (3 \times 3)$$
$$= 2401 \times 9$$
$$= 21,609$$

**Dividing Like Bases: A Shortcut**
This shortcut can save you time and effort when two like bases are to be divided. First, determine a new exponent by subtracting the exponent of the divisor from the exponent of the dividend. Then, using the new exponent, raise the common base number to its power. Let's look at a couple of examples. (Remember, unlike bases cannot be divided using this shortcut.)

**EXAMPLE 1:** *Divide $6^5$ by $6^3$.*

$$6^5 \div 6^3 = 6^{5-3}$$
$$= 6^2$$
$$= 36$$

**EXAMPLE 2:** *Divide $1.5^8$ by $1.5^5$.*
$$1.5^8 \div 1.5^5 = 1.5^{8-5}$$
$$= 1.5^3$$
$$= 3.375$$

**EXAMPLE 3:** *Divide $5^4$ by $2^3$.*
The bases are unlike numbers (5 and 2), so you can't use the shortcut. Instead, you must determine each power, then do the necessary division.

$$5^4 \div 2^3 = (5 \times 5 \times 5 \times 5) \div (2 \times 2 \times 2)$$
$$= 625 \div 8$$
$$= 78.125$$

## Understanding Roots

The *root* of any number can be defined as a factor that, when repeatedly multiplied, produces the number. For example, a root of 81 is 3, since the factor 3, when repeatedly multiplied, produces 81 ($3 \times 3 \times 3 \times 3 = 81$). A root of 3125 is 5, since the factor 5, when repeatedly multiplied, will yield 3125 ($5 \times 5 \times 5 \times 5 \times 5 = 3125$).

### Square Root

The *square root* of a number is a factor that when multiplied twice produces the number. For example, the square root of 9 is 3, since the factor 3 multiplied twice produces 9 ($3 \times 3 = 9$). The square root of 16 is 4, since $4 \times 4 = 16$.

### Cube Root

The *cube root* of a number is a factor that when multiplied three times produces the number. For example, the cube root of 8 is 2, since the factor 2 multiplied three times produces 8 ($2 \times 2 \times 2 = 8$). The cube root of 216 is 6, since $6 \times 6 \times 6 = 216$.

### The Radical Sign

A special symbol ($\sqrt{\phantom{xx}}$) called a *radical sign* is used to indicate the root of a number. A small raised number to the left of the radical sign, called an *index*, indicates how many times the equal factors are multiplied to produce the number. Therefore, $^3\sqrt{125}$ indicates the cube root of 125, and $^4\sqrt{81}$ indicates the fourth root of 81. A radical sign without an index number represents the square root of the number. For example, $\sqrt{64}$ means the square root of 64, and $\sqrt{100}$ indicates the square root of 100.

### Roots as Fractions or Decimals

Up to this point, all the roots we've looked at have been nice, round whole numbers. However, as you might expect, arithmetic is rarely this perfect. Indeed, the roots of most numbers include fractions or decimals. For example, the cube root of 6 ($6^3$) is 1.81712 and the square root of 8 ($\sqrt{8}$) is 2.82843. However, beyond the fact that roots with fractions and decimals have a few more digits, the basic procedure for using them remains the same.

## Finding the Roots of a Number

You will recall from earlier in this chapter that you use an exponent and a base number in order to find the power of a number. The procedure for finding the root of a number is the reverse process. Here, since the power is known, you use an exponent and the power to find the root. There are several ways to determine the roots of a number. Let's look at the ones most commonly used.

### Finding Roots by Estimating

You can find the root of a number by doing a series of estimates. This procedure can be a bit slow, but it eventually gets the job done. Here are a couple examples.

### EXAMPLE 1: *Find $\sqrt{34}$.*

Start by making a guess. Pick a number that, when squared, will be close to 34. Let's choose 5.

$$5 \times 5 = 25$$

Too small, so try 6.

$$6 \times 6 = 36$$

Too big. Try 5.5, a number midway between 5 and 6.

$$5.5 \times 5.5 = 30.25$$

Too small. Try 5.8.
$$5.8 \times 5.8 = 33.64$$

Still too small, but getting close. Try 5.85.

$$5.85 \times 5.85 = 34.2225$$

A little too big, try 5.83.

$$5.83 \times 5.83 = 33.9889$$

The root is still a bit small, but it should be close enough for any woodworking application. Therefore, $\sqrt{34} = 5.83$.

**EXAMPLE 2: *Find $\sqrt[4]{128}$.***

Start by making a guess. Let's say 3.

$$3 \times 3 \times 3 \times 3 = 81$$

Too small, so try 4.

$$4 \times 4 \times 4 \times 4 = 256$$

Too big. Try 3.5, a number midway between 3 and 4.

$$3.5 \times 3.5 \times 3.5 \times 3.5 = 150.0625$$

Too big, try 3.3.

$$3.3 \times 3.3 \times 3.3 \times 3.3 = 118.5921$$

A little small, but getting close. Try 3.36.

$$3.36 \times 3.36 \times 3.36 \times 3.36 = 127.45506$$

This is likely to be close enough for any woodworking application, but if you want it a bit closer, try 3.364.

$$3.364 \times 3.364 \times 3.364 \times 3.364 = 128.06308$$

That's pretty darn close—no need to go further. Therefore, $\sqrt[4]{128} = 3.364$.

## Finding Roots by Using a Table

Most good math books include a table that lists the square and cube roots of many numbers. Indeed, a table with square and cube roots appears in the appendix of this book. Clearly, such a table will get you a root much faster than using the estimating method, as long as the number you are working with is listed in the table.

**EXAMPLE 1: *Find the cube root of 51 ($\sqrt[3]{51}$).***
Referring to the table in the appendix, the cube root of 51 is 3.70843.

**EXAMPLE 2: *What is the square root of $\frac{9}{32}$ ($\sqrt{\frac{9}{32}}$)?***
Referring to the table in the appendix, the square root of $\frac{9}{32}$ is .530330.

## Finding Roots by Using a Calculator

Most calculators on the market today—even the most basic types—have a square root key that enables you to quickly find the square root of a number. Simply punch in the number and hit the square root key. The number displayed is the square root.

**EXAMPLE: *Find the square root of 257 ($\sqrt{257}$).***
Using a calculator with a square root key, punch in the number 257 then hit the square root key. The number displayed, 16.031219, is the square root.

Specialized calculators, such as scientific calculators, also include keys that allow easy calculation of cube roots and other roots.

# Part Two

# BASIC WOODSHOP GEOMETRY

CHAPTER 6

# *Common Geometric Shapes*

In geometry, there are two basic types of shapes: those that have a *plane figure* and those that have a *solid figure*. Plane figures have length and width, but no depth. Examples include squares, rectangles, triangles, hexagons and circles. Solid figures have length, width and depth. Examples include prisms, cylinders, cones and spheres.

   This chapter will introduce some of the plane and solid figures that you might encounter in the woodshop. Once you can recognize the basic geometric shapes, you'll be able to do all sorts of useful things. For example, when you know that a tabletop you are building has a rectangular shape, it will be easy to calculate the surface area or the volume. Armed with that information, you will see in later chapters how to determine the number of board feet of stock needed or how much polyurethane you must need to buy in order to apply three coats to all surfaces. You'll even be able to figure out, if need be, how much the top weighs.

## Plane Figures

Let's begin by looking at some of the plane geometric figures that you commonly find in the workshop.

### Lines

Since geometric figures are made up of lines, it's helpful to be able to recognize and name them.

**STRAIGHT LINE**

The shortest distance between two points. (The term *line,* unless further defined, means a straight line.)

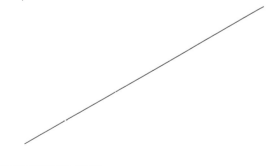

**HORIZONTAL LINE**

A line parallel to the horizon.

**VERTICAL LINE**
A line perpendicular to the horizon.

**OBLIQUE LINE**
A line that is neither horizontal nor vertical.

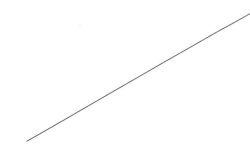

**PERPENDICULAR LINE**
A line that intersects another line at 90°.

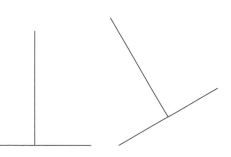

**PARALLEL LINES**
Two or more lines that remain the same distance apart at all points.

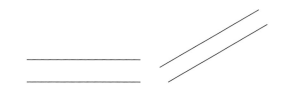

**IRREGULAR CURVED LINES**
A curved line with a radius that constantly changes.

## Angles

When two lines meet, the space between them is called an *angle*. The two lines are called the *angle sides* and the point where they meet is called the *vertex*. An angle is usually measured in degrees. The various types of angles you're likely to come across in the woodshop are shown here.

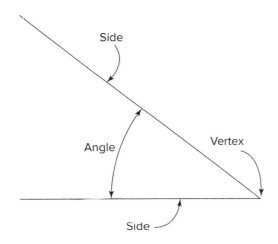

Side

Angle          Vertex

Side

### STRAIGHT ANGLE

Two lines that intersect to form a straight line. A straight line angle measures 180°.

### RIGHT ANGLE

The angle formed by a line perpendicular to another line. A right angle measures 90°.

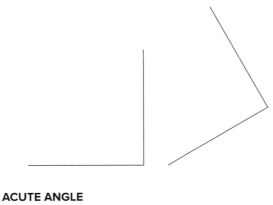

### ACUTE ANGLE

An angle that is less than 90°.

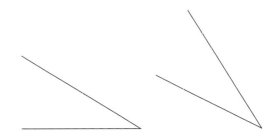

### OBTUSE ANGLE

An angle that is more than 90° but less than 180°.

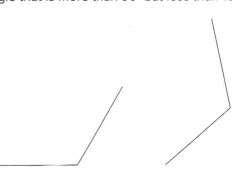

Part Two
BASIC WOODSHOP GEOMETRY

### Polygons

A *polygon* is a closed plane figure that has three or more sides and angles. A polygon that has all angles equal and all sides equal in length is called a *regular polygon.* Polygons are usually named according to the number of sides they have. Some of the polygons are:

| NAME | NUMBER OF SIDES |
|------|------|
| Triangle | 3 |
| Quadrilateral | 4 |
| Pentagon | 5 |
| Hexagon | 6 |
| Octagon | 8 |
| Decagon | 10 |
| Dodecagon | 12 |

### TRIANGLES

A polygon with three sides and three angles is called a *triangle.* It's not uncommon to come across triangle shapes in the workshop. For example, bevels, tapers, wedges, dovetails and gussets—to name a few—all have triangular shapes.

### RIGHT TRIANGLE

A triangle with one 90° angle.

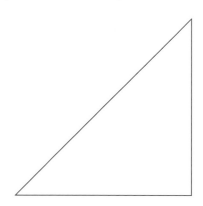

### EQUILATERAL TRIANGLE

A triangle whose sides are of equal length.

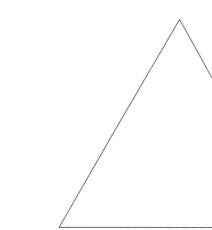

### ISOCELES TRIANGLE
A triangle with two sides of equal length.

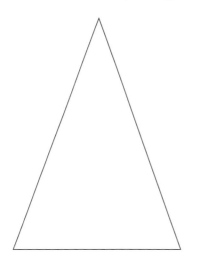

### SCALENE TRIANGLE
A triangle with all sides unequal in length.

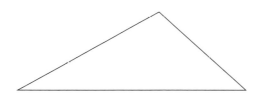

### OBTUSE TRIANGLE
A triangle with an obtuse angle.

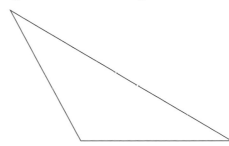

## Quadrilaterals
A polygon with four sides and four angles is called a *quadrilateral*. In a quadrilateral, the sum of the four angles is always equal to 360°.

Quadrilaterals abound in the woodshop. You'll find that most tabletops have a square or rectangular shape. I've seen drafting tables with leg frames in the shape of a trapezoid. I once worked on an outdoor playhouse that had louvers cut to produce a rhomboid-shaped cross section.

### RECTANGLE
A quadrilateral with four right angles.

### SQUARE

A quadrilateral with four right angles and four equal-length sides.

### RHOMBOID

A quadrilateral with opposite sides parallel, adjacent sides unequal, and usually having two acute angles and two obtuse angles.

### RHOMBUS

A quadrilateral with all sides equal in length, opposite sides parallel, and usually having two acute angles and two obtuse angles.

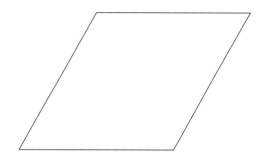

### TRAPEZOID

A quadrilateral with two sides parallel and two sides not parallel.

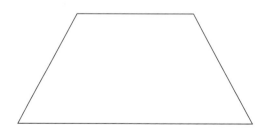

### TRAPEZIUM

A quadrilateral having no sides parallel.

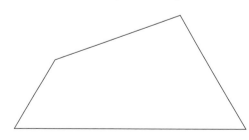

## Other Polygons

Several other polygon shapes seem to regularly show up in the woodshop. Many old-time schoolhouse clocks are made using an octagon shape for the frame. Tabletops are sometimes made in the shape of a pentagon. I once built a display pedestal with a base that was shaped like a hexagon.

### REGULAR PENTAGON

A figure having five equal-length sides and five equal angles.

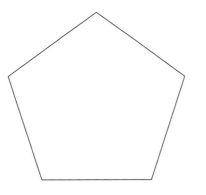

### REGULAR HEXAGON

A figure having six equal-length sides and six equal angles.

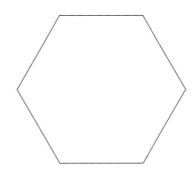

### REGULAR OCTAGON

A figure having eight equal-length sides and eight right angles.

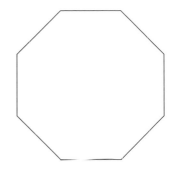

*Part Two*
**BASIC WOODSHOP GEOMETRY**

### REGULAR DECAGON
A figure having ten equal-length sides and ten equal angles.

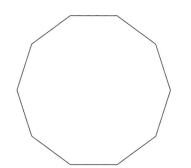

### REGULAR DODECAGON
A figure having twelve equal-length sides and twelve equal angles.

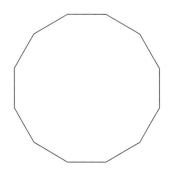

## Circles
All the shapes we have looked at so far have sides constructed from straight lines. But the circle is also an important part of geometry. Indeed, in the woodshop, circles are used to construct tabletops, toy wheels, clock faces, round mirrors and much more. Of course, you'll see a circle when you look at a drilled hole or the end of any dowel, round table leg or lathe turning. Let's consider the circle and some of its related components.

### CIRCLE
A closed curve with all points equal distance from the center point.

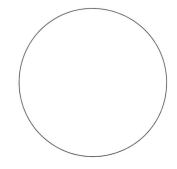

**BASIC WOODSHOP GEOMETRY**   *Part Two*

### CONCENTRIC CIRCLES
Two or more circles with the same center point but with different diameters.

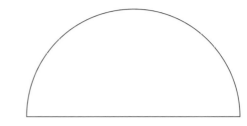

### ECCENTRIC CIRCLES
Two or more intersecting circles with different center points.

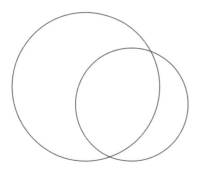

### SEMICIRCLE
A half of a circle.

### CIRCUMFERENCE
The distance around a circle.

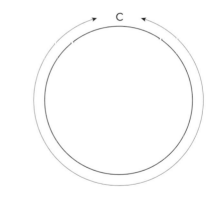

C – Circumference

Part Two
BASIC WOODSHOP GEOMETRY

### ARC

A portion of the circumference.

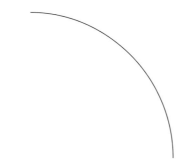

### RADIUS

A straight line extending from the center of a circle to any point on the circle.

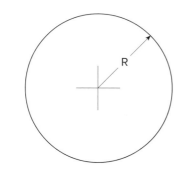

R = Radius

### DIAMETER

A straight line that passes through the center of a circle and extends from one side of the circle to the other.

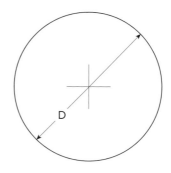

D = Diameter

### CHORD

A straight line connecting two points on a circle.

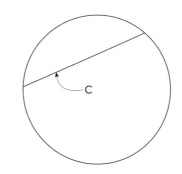

C = Chord

Part Two
BASIC WOODSHOP GEOMETRY

### TANGENT

A straight line that touches a circle at only one point.

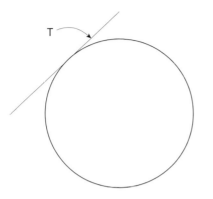

T = Tangent

### SEGMENT

That part of a circle (or geometric figure) cut off by a straight line.

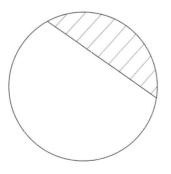

### ELLIPSES

An *ellipse* is a diagonal section of a cone, which is neither parallel nor perpendicular to the base of the cone. Dining tables are sometimes cut into the shape of an ellipses. The oval-shaped curve adds an interesting shape to the top and allows for comfortable seating around the table.

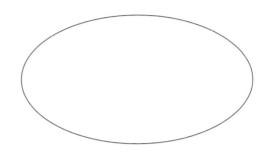

## Solid Figures

Here are some of the solid geometric figures you'll commonly find in the woodshop. In some cases, I'm afraid the definitions are almost painful to read, but I felt it best to include them anyway. Although you might not remember the definitions, I suspect you'll find that the illustrations quickly clear up any confusion.

### Prisms

A *prism* is a solid with two parallel bases that are identical polygons. The prism ends are called *bases,* while the prism sides are called the *lateral faces.* A prism can be square, rectangular, triangular, pentagonal, and so on, according to the shape of the base.

**RIGHT SQUARE PRISM**
A prism with lateral faces perpendicular to square bases.

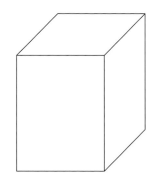

**RIGHT RECTANGULAR PRISM**
A prism with lateral faces perpendicular to rectangular bases.

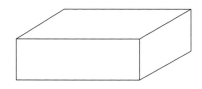

**CUBE OR HEXAHEDRON**
A prism with bases and lateral faces that are squares.

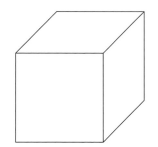

**OBLIQUE RECTANGULAR PRISM**
A prism with lateral faces not perpendicular to rectangular bases.

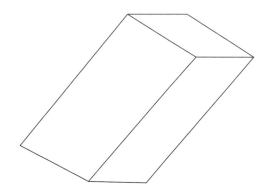

*Part Two*
**BASIC WOODSHOP GEOMETRY**

### TRIANGULAR PRISM

A prism with triangular bases.

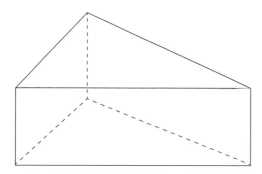

### OBLIQUE CYLINDER

A cylinder with the axis not perpendicular to the base.

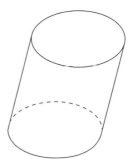

## Cylinders

Strictly defined, a *cylinder* is a solid bounded by two equal, parallel circles and by a curved surface formed by moving a straight line of fixed length so the ends lie on the two parallel circles. Ouch! If a more palatable definition seems in order, let's simply say a cylinder has a shape like a can of soup.

### RIGHT CYLINDER

A cylinder with the axis perpendicular to the bases. (The axis is the central line of any symmetrical or nearly symmetrical body.)

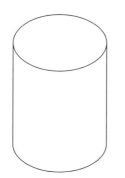

## Cones

A *cone* is a solid with a circular base and a surface that narrows to a point at the top.

### RIGHT CONE

A cone whose axis is perpendicular to the base.

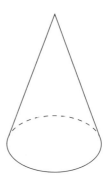

### OBLIQUE CONE

A cone whose axis is not perpendicular to the base.

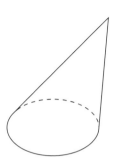

### TRUNCATED RIGHT CONE

The portion remaining after a cutting plane is passed through a right cone.

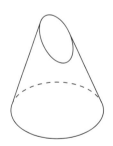

## Pyramids

A solid with a polygon for its base and triangles for its sides is called a *pyramid*.

### RIGHT SQUARE PYRAMID

A pyramid whose axis is perpendicular to a square base.

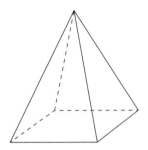

## Oblique Square Pyramid

A pyramid whose axis is not perpendicular to a square base.

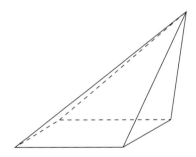

### RIGHT RECTANGULAR PYRAMID
A pyramid whose axis is perpendicular to a rectangular base.

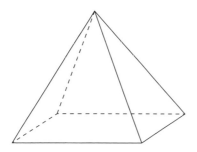

### RIGHT TRIANGULAR PYRAMID
A pyramid whose axis is perpendicular to a triangular base.

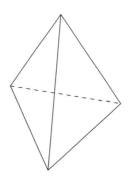

### TRUNCATED PYRAMID
The portion remaining after a cutting plane is passed through a pyramid.

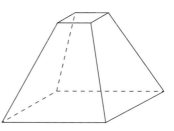

### Sphere
A sphere is a round solid figure in which every point on the surface is the same distance from the center.

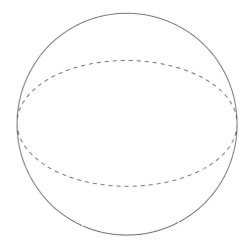

*Part Two*
**BASIC WOODSHOP GEOMETRY**

CHAPTER 7

# Plane Figure Formulas

Plane figures, you will recall from chapter six, have length and width, but no depth. This chapter provides formulas for calculating both the area and the distance around each of the plane figures introduced in chapter six.

The amount of surface that a shape has is called its *area* or *surface area*. Square units of measurements (square inches, square feet, square millimeters, square meters, etc.) are used to describe area.

The distance around any closed plane figure is called the *perimeter,* while the distance around a circle is commonly called the *circumference*. Perimeter and circumference are described using linear units of measurement (inches, feet, millimeters, centimeters and the like).

## Triangle

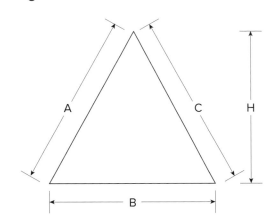

Area = ½ B × H
H = Height of the triangle
Perimeter = A + B + C

## Square

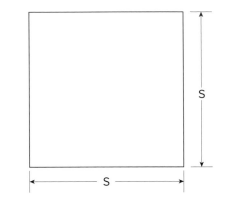

Area = $S^2$
Perimeter = 4 × S

## Rectangle

Area = L × W
Perimeter = (2 × L) + (2 × W)

## Rhomboid

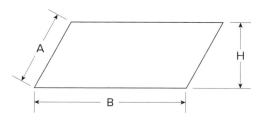

Area = B × H
where:
H = Height of the rhomboid
Perimeter = (2 × A) + (2 × B)

## Rhombus

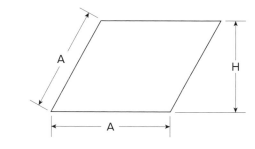

Area = A × H
where:
H = Height of the rhombus
Perimeter = 4 × A

## Trapezoid

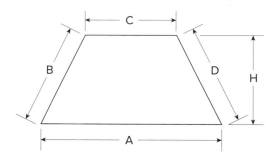

$$\text{Area} = \frac{(A + C) \times H}{2}$$

Perimeter = A + B + C + D

*Part Two*
**BASIC WOODSHOP GEOMETRY**

## Trapezium

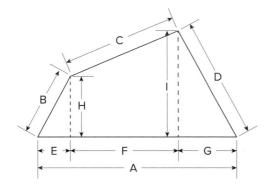

$$\text{Area} = \frac{[(H + I) \times F] + (E \times H) + (G \times I)}{2}$$

$$\text{Perimeter} = A + B + C + D$$

## Regular Pentagon

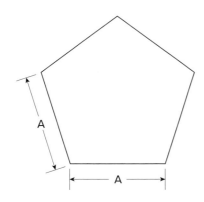

Area = 1.7205 × A²
Perimeter = 5 × A

## Regular Hexagon

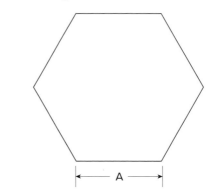

Area = 2.5981 × A²
Perimeter = 6 × A

## Regular Octagon

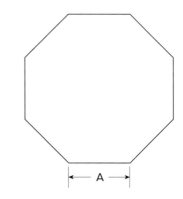

Area = 4.8284 × A²
Perimeter = 8 × A

*Part Two*
BASIC WOODSHOP GEOMETRY

## Regular Decagon

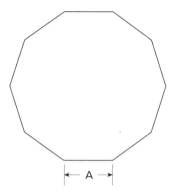

Area = 7.6924 × A²
Perimeter = 10 × A

## Regular Dodecagon

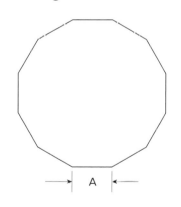

Area = 11.1961 × A²
Perimeter = 12 × A

## Ellipse

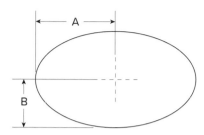

Area = 3.14159 × A × B
Perimeter (approximate) =
3.14159 [1.5(A + B) − √A × B]

## Circle

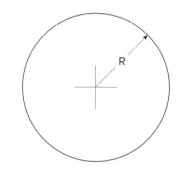

Area = 3.14159 × R²
where:
R = Radius of the circle
Circumference = 6.2832 × R

*Part Two*
BASIC WOODSHOP GEOMETRY

## *Using the Area Formula*

A woodshop floor measuring 15' by 20' is to be covered with pine flooring. According to the flooring supplier, 1.38 board feet of pine is needed for each square foot of floor. How many board feet of flooring must be ordered?

**Step 1:** Calculate the area of the floor in square feet. Since the floor has the shape of a rectangle, use the formula for the area of a rectangle.
Area = L × W
Area = 20' × 15'
Area = 300 square feet

**Step 2:** Multiply the area of the floor (in square feet) by 1.38 to determine how many board feet of flooring are needed.
300 × 1.38 = 414 board feet

## *Using the Perimeter Formula*

A tabletop is made from ¾"-thick walnut plywood is to measure 48" by 48" when finished. The plywood requires an edging made from ¾" by ¾" walnut stock. The ends of the edging are mitered. How many feet of edging are needed?

**Step 1:** Calculate the perimeter of the tabletop. Since the tabletop has the shape of a square, use the formula for the perimeter of a square.
Area = 4 × S
Area = 4 × 48"
Perimeter = 192"

**Step 2:** Convert inches to feet (see conversion table in appendix).
192" × .08333 = 16'

# CHAPTER 8
# *Solid Figure Formulas*

From chapter six, you know that a solid figure has three dimensions: length, width and depth. Two important measurements of a solid figure are volume and surface area. *Volume* is a measure of the three-dimensional size of a solid figure. *Surface area,* you will recall from chapter seven, is a measure of the amount of surface on the figure. This chapter provides formulas for calculating the volume and surface area for several of the solid figures shown in chapter six. Volume is measured in cubic units (cubic inches, cubic feet, cubic millimeters, cubic meters, etc.). Surface area is measured in square units (square inches, square feet, square millimeters, square meters, etc.).

## Cube (also called a Hexahedron)

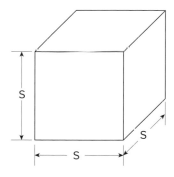

Volume = $S^3$
Surface Area = $6 \times S^2$
where:
S = Side length

## Right Rectangular Prism

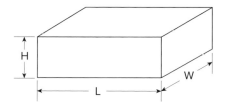

Volume = L × W × H
Surface Area = 2(L × W) ⏐ 2(W × H) + 2(L × H)
where:
L = Prism length
W = Prism width
H = Prism height

## Right Cylinder

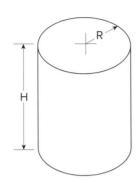

Volume = $3.14159 \times R^2 \times H$
Surface Area = $(6.28318 \times R) \times (R + H)$
where:
R = Radius of cylinder
H = Height of cylinder

## Right Cone

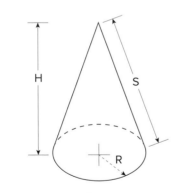

Volume = $\dfrac{3.14159 \times R^2 \times H}{3}$

Surface Area = $3.14159 \times R \times (R + S)$
where:
R = Radius of base
H = Height of cone
S = Length of side
Note: H is perpendicular to the base.

## Right Square Pyramid

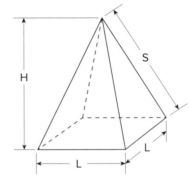

Volume = $\dfrac{L^2 \times H}{3}$

Surface Area = $(2 \times L \times S) + L^2$
where:
L = Base length
H = Height of pyramid
S = Side length
Note: H is perpendicular to the base.

## Right Rectangular Pyramid

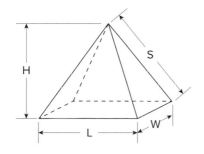

$$\text{Volume} = \frac{L \times W \times H}{3}$$

Surface Area = LS + WS + LW
where:
L = Base length
W = Base width
H = Height of pyramid
S = Side length
Note: H is perpendicular to the base.

## Right Pyramid (General Formula)

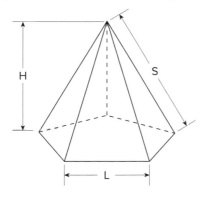

$$\text{Volume} = \frac{(\text{Area of Base}) \times H}{3}$$

$$\text{Surface Area} = \frac{(\text{Perimeter of Base}) \times S}{2} + \text{Area of Base}$$

where:
H = Height of pyramid
S = Side length
Note: H is perpendicular to the base.

## Sphere

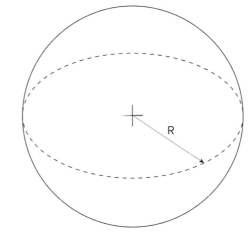

Volume = $4.1888 \times R^3$
Surface Area = $12.5664 \times R^2$
where:
R = Radius of sphere

*Part Two*
**BASIC WOODSHOP GEOMETRY**

# *Using the Surface Area Formula*

The top of a dining table measures 1½" thick by 3' wide by 7' long. The top requires three coats of varnish. How much varnish is needed if it covers at a rate of 100 square feet per quart?

**Step 1:** Determine the surface area of the tabletop (in square feet). Since the tabletop has the shape of a right rectangular prism, use the formula:

Surface Area = 2(L × W) + 2(W × H) + 2(L × H)
L = length = 7'
W = width = 3'
H = height = 1½"

**Step 2:** Convert the 1½" height (H) to feet (see conversion tables in appendix) so all the dimensions have the same unit of measurement.
H = 1½" × .08333 = .125'

**Step 3:** Calculate the surface area using the formula.
Surface Area = 2(L × W) + 2(W × H) + 2(L × H)
Surface Area =2(7 × 3) + 2(3 × .125) + 2(7 × .125)
Surface Area = 2(21) + 2(.375) + 2(.875)
Surface Area = 42 + .75 + 1.75
Surface Area = 44.5 square feet

**Step 4:** Determine the total surface area to be covered by 3 coats of varnish.
3 coats × 44.5 square feet = 133.5 square feet
Since the varnish covers at a rate of 100 square feet per quart, you'll need just under 1½ quarts (133.5 ÷ 100 = 1.335) to complete the job.

*Part Two*

BASIC WOODSHOP GEOMETRY

CHAPTER 9

# *Basic Geometric Construction*

In the woodshop, it's often helpful to be able to quickly sketch a portion of a project or even a wood joint. The various geometric construction techniques shown here can save you time and effort whenever a quick sketch is in order. You'll find they can be done with a minimum of tools. Indeed, for most of the constructions, you'll need only a couple of drafting triangles, a straightedge and a compass.

   In this chapter you'll also find that you can use geometric constructions to create some interesting patterns that are perfect for inlaying, chip carving or decorating painted furniture. Several of the patterns shown are commonly used to decorate furniture in the Pennsylvania Dutch style.

   Finally, this chapter shows you how to quickly create a number of different angles using only a couple of drafting triangles and a T-square.

## The Basic Constructions Step by Step

I've always enjoyed working with drafting tools, so I find it fun to do these constructions. It's also the best way to get familiar with them, so sharpen the pencil point on your compass, collect some scrap paper and go to work.

### Bisecting a Straight Line

To bisect a straight line is to divide the line in half. Either a compass or a drafting triangle can be used for this.

**COMPASS METHOD**

**Step 1:** Set the compass for any radius greater than the length of AB.

**Step 2:** With points A and B as centers, use the compass to mark intersecting arcs at C and D.

**Step 3:** Draw a straight line through points C and D to bisect the line AB.

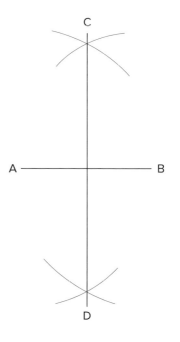

## DRAFTING TRIANGLE METHOD

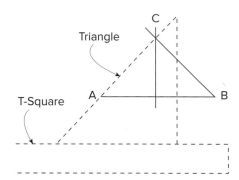

## Trisecting a Straight Line

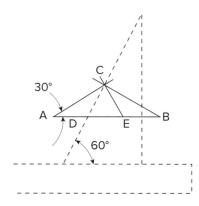

**Step 1:** Tape paper to drafting board.

**Step 2:** Use the T-square to draw line AB.

**Step 3:** With the T-square and a 45° (or 60°) drafting triangle, draw lines through points A and B to create point C.

**Step 4:** Draw a straight line perpendicular to AB through point C to bisect line AB.

To trisect a straight line is to divide the line into thirds. You'll need the T-square and a 30° x 60° drafting triangle to do the work.

**Step 1:** Tape paper to drafting board.

**Step 2:** Use the T-square to draw line AB.

**Step 3:** Draw two lines at 30°: one through point A and one through point B.

**Step 4:** Mark the intersection of the two lines as point C.

**Step 5:** Draw two lines at 60° through point C to line AB.

**Step 6:** To complete the trisection, mark the intersection of the lines as points D and E. Line AD = line DE = line EB.

*Part Two*
BASIC WOODSHOP GEOMETRY

## Bisecting an Arc

To bisect an arc is to find the arc's midpoint.

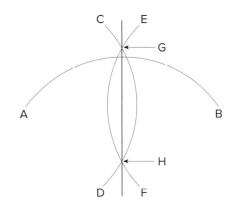

**Step 1:** Set the compass for any radius greater than one-half the length of arc AB.

**Step 2:** With point A as the center, scribe arc CD.

**Step 3:** With point B as the center, scribe arc EF.

**Step 4:** Mark the points of intersection of arcs CD and EF as G and H.

**Step 5:** To complete the bisection, draw a straight line connecting points G and H.

## Bisecting an Angle

To bisect an angle is to divide the angle in half.

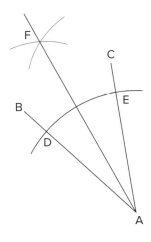

**Step 1:** Label points A (the vertex), B and C on the angle.

**Step 2:** With point A as the center, use the compass to scribe an arc that intersects the angle sides at D and E.

**Step 3:** Set the compass for any radius greater than the length of chord DE.

**Step 4:** Use the compass to scribe a pair of intersecting lines, one with point D as a center, one with point E as the center. Label the intersection as point F.

**Step 5:** Draw line AF to bisect the angle.

*Part Two*

**BASIC WOODSHOP GEOMETRY**

## Drawing an Angle Equal to Another Angle

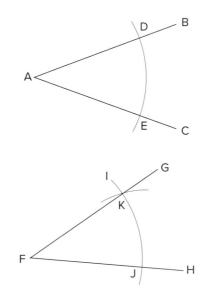

**Step 1:** Label points A (the vertex), B and C on the angle.

**Step 2:** Draw line FH to represent one side of the new angle.

**Step 3:** With point A as the center, use the compass to scribe an arc that intersects the angle sides at D and E.

**Step 4:** With the compass at the same radius, and with point F on the new triangle as the center, scribe a long arc that intersects line FH at J.

**Step 5:** Set the compass to a radius that equals the length of chord DE.

**Step 6:** With point J as the center, scribe an arc to intersect arc IJ at K.

**Step 7:** Draw line FG through K to complete the angle.

## Drawing an Equilateral Triangle

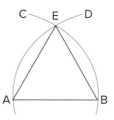

**Step 1:** Draw line AB to represent the length of one side of the triangle.

**Step 2:** Set the compass for a radius that equals the length of line AB.

**Step 3:** With point A as the center, scribe the arc BC.

**Step 4:** With point B as the center, scribe the arc AD.

**Step 5:** Mark the point where the arcs intersect as E.

**Step 6:** To complete the equilateral triangle, draw straight lines connecting points A and E and points B and E.

*Part Two*
**BASIC WOODSHOP GEOMETRY**

## Drawing a Square When Given the Diagonal

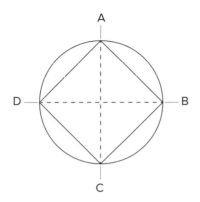

**Step 1:** Using the compass, scribe a circle with a diameter that is equal to the length of the diagonal.

**Step 2:** Extend the two perpendicular center lines to the edge of the circle.

**Step 3:** Mark the four points where the center lines intersect the circle as A, B, C and D.

**Step 4:** To complete the square, draw a straight line connecting points A and B, B and C, C and D, and D and A.

## Drawing a Square When Given the Side

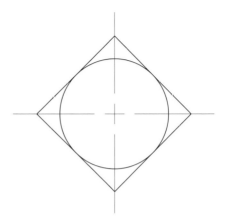

**Step 1:** Use the compass to scribe a circle with a diameter that is equal to the length of the side.

**Step 2:** Extend two perpendicular center lines to the edge of the circle.

**Step 3:** Use a 45° triangle to draw four straight lines, each one tangent to the circle and at 45° to the center lines.

**BASIC WOODSHOP GEOMETRY**

## Drawing a Regular Pentagon

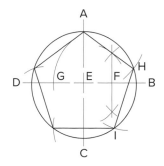

**Step 1:** Use the compass to scribe a circle, then draw two perpendicular center lines.

**Step 2:** Mark the four points where the center lines intersect the circle as A, B, C and D.

**Step 3:** Mark the center point of the circle as E.

**Step 4:** Bisect the line EB. Mark the midpoint of line EB as F.

**Step 5:** Set the compass for a radius that equals the length of FA.

**Step 6:** Using point F as the center point, scribe the arc AG.

**Step 7:** Set the compass for a radius that equals the length of AG.

**Step 8:** Starting with point A as a center point, use the compass to scribe an arc that intersects the circle at H. Next, with point H as the center point, scribe an arc that intersects at I. Continue this procedure two more times to complete a total of five points on the circle.

**Step 9:** To complete the pentagon, draw five straight lines to connect the five points on the circle.

## Drawing a Regular Hexagon

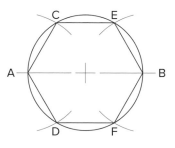

**Step 1:** Use the compass to draw a circle.

**Step 2:** Draw two perpendicular center lines and mark points A and B.

**Step 3:** Without changing the compass setting, use point A as a center point to scribe arcs locating points C and D.

**Step 4:** Using point B as a center point, scribe arcs to locate points E and F.

**Step 5:** To complete the hexagon, draw six straight lines to connect the six points on the circle.

## Drawing a Regular Octagon

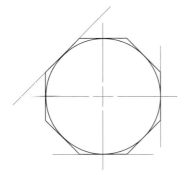

**Step 1:** Use the compass to draw a circle, then draw two perpendicular center lines.

**Step 2:** Use a 45° triangle to draw four straight lines, each one tangent to the circle and 45° to the center lines.

**Step 3:** Use a 90° triangle to draw two straight vertical lines tangent to the circle.

**Step 4:** To complete the octagon, use the T-square to draw two straight horizontal lines tangent to the circle.

## Drawing a Regular Polygon

A decagon is used here as an example, but the same basic procedure can be applied to any regular polygon.

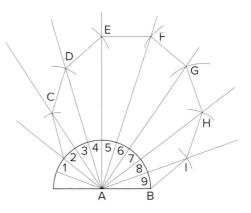

**Step 1:** Draw line AB representing the length of one side of the polygon.

**Step 2:** Set the compass for a radius that equals the length AB.

**Step 3:** With point A as a center point, draw a semicircle.

**Step 4:** Divide the semicircle into equal parts. The number of equal parts must equal the number of polygon sides. For a decagon—a ten-sided polygon—the semicircle is divided into ten parts. A semicircle has 180°, so 180° ÷ 10 = 18° in each equal part. Use a protractor to mark points on the semicircle at 18°, 36°, 54°, 72°, 90°, 108°, 126°, 144° and 162°. Label the points 1 through 9, as shown.

**Step 5:** Draw an extended straight line from point A through point 2. Do the same for points 3 through 9.

**BASIC WOODSHOP GEOMETRY** *Part Two*

**Step 6:** With the compass still set for a radius that equals the length of AB, use point 2 as a center point and scribe an arc to intersect line A3. Mark this point as C.

**Step 7:** Use point C as a center point and scribe an arc to intersect line A4. Mark this point as D.

**Step 8:** Use point D as a center point and scribe an arc to intersect line A5. Mark this point as E. (You can continue working your way around the polygon to complete the layout, but the construction is likely to be more accurate if the next step begins at point B.)

**Step 9:** Use point B as a center point and scribe an arc to intersect line A9. Mark this point as I.

**Step 10:** Use point I as a center point and scribe an arc to intersect line AB. Mark this point as H.

**Step 11:** Use point H as a center point and scribe an arc to intersect line A7. Mark this point as G.

**Step 12:** Use point G as a center point and scribe an arc to intersect line A6. Mark this point as F.

**Step 13:** To complete the decagon, connect points A, 2, C, D, E, F, G, H, I and B.

## Drawing an Arc Tangent to a Right Angle

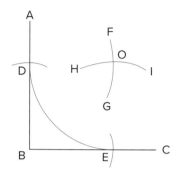

**Step 1:** Draw line AB at a right angle to line BC.

**Step 2:** Set the compass to equal the radius of the desired arc.

**Step 3:** Use point B as a center point and scribe an arc that intersects lines AB and BC. Label points of intersection D and E.

**Step 4:** With the same compass setting, use point D as a center point and scribe arc FG.

**Step 5:** With the same compass setting, use point E as a center point and scribe arc HI. Mark the intersection of arcs FG and HI as O.

**Step 6:** With the same compass setting, use point O as a center point and scribe the arc connecting points D and E. The arc is tangent to the right angle at D and E.

Part Two
BASIC WOODSHOP GEOMETRY

## Drawing an Arc Tangent to an Acute Angle

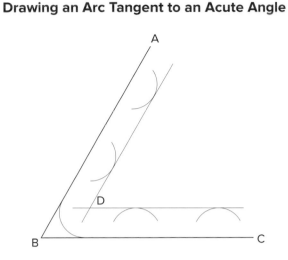

**Step 1:** Draw line AB at an acute angle to line BC.

**Step 2:** Set the compass to equal the radius of the desired arc.

**Step 3:** Select a point near each end of lines AB and BC as center points, then scribe an arc at each point.

**Step 4:** Draw lines tangent to the arcs.

**Step 5:** Mark the intersection of the lines as point D.

**Step 6:** Without changing the compass setting, use point D as a center point and scribe an arc connecting lines AB and BC. The arc is tangent to the acute angle formed by lines AB and BC.

## Drawing an Arc Tangent to an Obtuse Angle

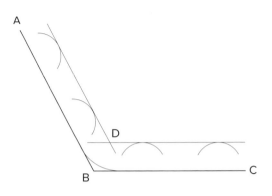

**Step 1:** Draw line AB at an obtuse angle to line BC.

**Step 2:** Set the compass to equal the radius of the desired arc.

**Step 3:** Select a point near each end of lines AB and BC as center points, then scribe an arc at each point.

**Step 4:** Draw lines tangent to the arcs.

**Step 5:** Mark the intersection of the lines as point D.

**Step 6:** Without changing the compass setting, use point D as a center point and scribe an arc connecting lines AB and BC. The arc is tangent to the acute angle formed by lines AB and BC.

## Drawing an Ellipse

An ellipse can be drawn using any one of several geometric construction methods. The method used here, called the *trammel method,* is particularly useful when you want to draw a full-size ellipse.

**Step 1:** Draw a horizontal line slightly larger than the ellipse length and a vertical line slightly longer than the ellipse width.

**Step 2:** Mark points X, Y and Z on a straightedge made from cardboard, stiff paper or a thin piece of wood. Make the length of XY equal to one-half the ellipse width. Make the length of XZ equal to one-half the ellipse length.

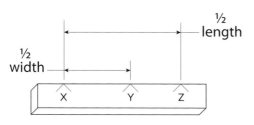

**Step 3:** Position the straightedge so that point Z falls at any point on the vertical line and point Y falls on the horizontal line. Hold the straightedge in position, then mark point X. The mark at point X represents a point on the perimeter of the ellipse.

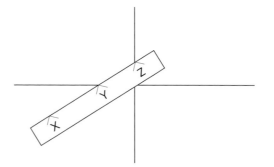

**Step 4:** Continue moving the straightedge, always keeping point Z on the vertical line and point Y on the horizontal line. Mark a new point X after each movement of the straightedge. Mark as many points as are needed to create a smooth curve along the entire perimeter of the ellipse.

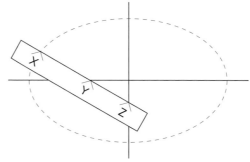

## Constructing Decorative Patterns Step by Step

With a little know-how and a compass, you can easily create some interesting patterns. All of these patterns can be put to good use on painted furniture. In addition, the heart-shaped pattern is often used as a decorative cutout on country furniture and accessories. Many chip carvers like to work with the five-point star and six-point petal flower.

### Drawing a Five-Point Star

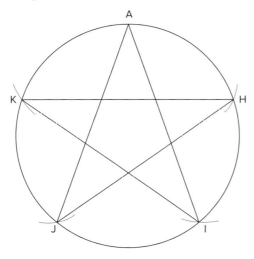

**Step 1:** Follow steps 1 through 8 in "Drawing a Regular Pentagon."

**Step 2:** Mark the points on the circle as A, H, I, J and K.

**Step 3:** Use a straight line to connect points A and I, A and J, H and K, H and J, and I and K.

### Drawing a Four-Point Star in a Square

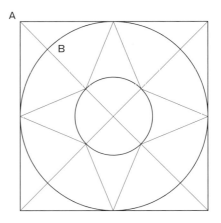

**Step 1:** Draw a square.

**Step 2:** Use straight lines to construct the diagonals.

**Step 3:** With the intersection of the diagonals as a center point, scribe a circle tangent to the sides of the square.

**Step 4:** Set the compass to equal length AB.

**Step 5:** With the intersection of the diagonals as a center point, use the compass to scribe a second circle inside the square.

**Step 6:** Connect the points of the star as shown.

## Drawing a Six-Petal Flower

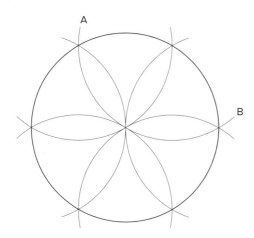

## Drawing a Triangle in a Circle

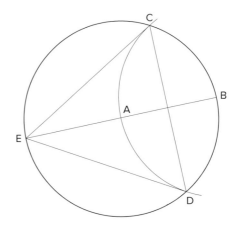

**Step 1:** Set the compass to equal the radius of the flower.

**Step 2:** Scribe the radius.

**Step 3:** Using any point on the diameter as a center point, scribe an arc that intersects the diameter at two points.

**Step 4:** Mark the intersections of the diameter as points A and B.

**Step 5:** With point A as a center point, use the same compass setting to scribe a second arc.

**Step 6:** With point B as a center point, use the same compass setting to scribe a third arc.

**Step 7:** Continue in this manner until all six petals are scribed.

**Step 1:** Set the compass to equal the radius of the desired diameter.

**Step 2:** Scribe the diameter and mark the center point as A.

**Step 3:** Select any point on the diameter and mark it as B.

**Step 4:** With point B as the center point, use the same compass setting to scribe an arc. Mark the points that the arc intersects the diameter as C and D.

**Step 5:** Use a straightedge to draw an extended line through points A and B. Mark the point that the line intersects the diameter as E.

**Step 6:** To complete the triangle, use the straightedge to connect points C, D and E.

*Part Two*
**BASIC WOODSHOP GEOMETRY**

## Drawing a Heart

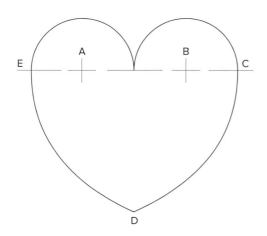

## Angles from Triangles

When used in combination, two triangles—a 45° and a 30° x 60°—can quickly create an assortment of commonly used angles.

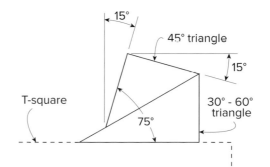

**Step 1:** Use the compass to scribe two semicircles tangent to each other. Mark the center points as A and B.

**Step 2:** Set the compass to equal the distance AC.

**Step 3:** With point A as a center point, scribe arc CD.

**Step 4:** To complete the heart, use point B as a center point and scribe arc ED.

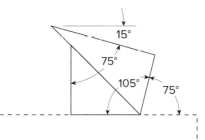

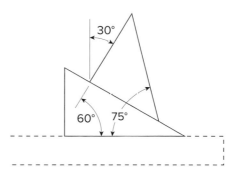

# CHAPTER 10

# Basic Geometric Theorems

In geometry, any statement or rule that can be proved to be true is called a *theorem*. An understanding of some of the basic theorems can often be helpful in the woodshop. Let's look at some of them.

*Part Two*
**BASIC WOODSHOP GEOMETRY**

When two lines intersect, the angles opposite each other are equal.

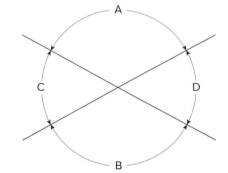

Angle A = Angle B
Angle C = Angle D

When a line intersects two parallel lines, the corresponding angles on each of the parallel lines are equal.

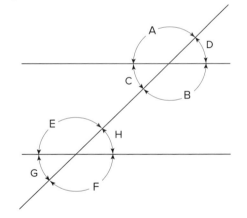

Angle A = Angle B = Angle E = Angle F
Angle C = Angle D = Angle G = Angle H

In any triangle, the sum of the three angles is 180°.

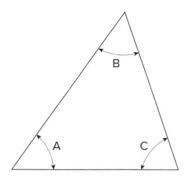

Angle A + Angle B + Angle C = 180°
Angle A = 180° − (Angle B + Angle C)
Angle B = 180° − (Angle A + Angle C)
Angle C = 180° − (Angle A + Angle B)

When a triangle has three sides equal in length (an equilateral angle), the three angles are equal (60°).

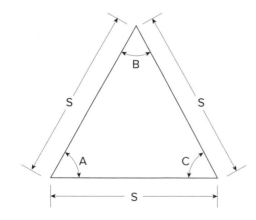

All sides (S) are the same length.
Therefore: Angle A = Angle B = Angle C = 60°

When a triangle has three 60° angles, the sides are equal in length and the triangle is an equilateral triangle.

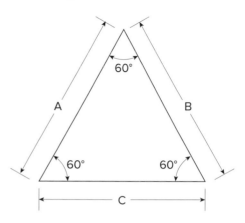

All angles are 60°
Therefore: Side A = Side B = Side C

When a triangle is equilateral, a line bisecting an angle also bisects the side opposite the angle. Also, the bisecting line is perpendicular to the side opposite the angle.

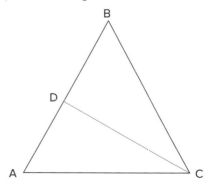

Line CD bisects Angle ACB
Therefore: Line AD = Line BD

Line CD is perpendicular to Line AB

When a triangle has two sides that are equal in length (an isosceles triangle), the angles opposite the two equal-length sides are also equal.

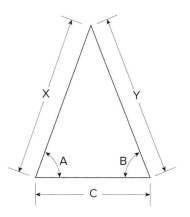

Side X = Side Y
Therefore: Angle A = Angle B

When a triangle has two angles that are equal, the sides opposite the two equal angles are equal in length.

Angle A = Angle B
Therefore: Side X = Side Y

When a triangle is isosceles, a line bisecting the angle formed by the intersection of the two equal-length sides bisects the side opposite that angle. Also, the bisecting line is perpendicular to the side opposite the angle.

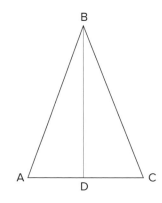

Line BD bisects Angle ABC
Therefore:
Line AD = Line DC
Line BD is perpendicular to Line AC

*Part Two*
**BASIC WOODSHOP GEOMETRY**

In any quadrilateral (four-sided figure), the sum of the four angles is 360°.

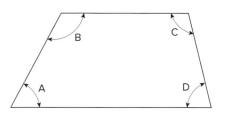

Angle A + Angle B + Angle C + Angle D = 360°
The equation can also be written as:
Angle A = 360° − (Angle B + Angle C + Angle D)
Angle B = 360° − (Angle A + Angle C + Angle D)
Angle C = 360° − (Angle A + Angle B + Angle D)
Angle D = 360° − (Angle A + Angle B + Angle C)

In any triangle, the exterior angle of a side is equal to the sum of the two opposite interior angles. (The exterior angle is the angle between a side of a triangle and a line extended from the adjacent side.)

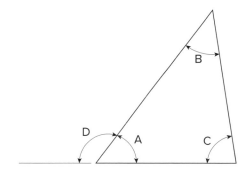

Angle D (the exterior angle) = Angle B + Angle C.

WOODSHOP APPLICATION

## Using a Geometric Theorem

One end of a 1 x 8 pine board is square cut; the other is cut at a 58° angle. What is the angle of B?

**Step 1:** Recognize that the beveled board has the shape of a quadrilateral.

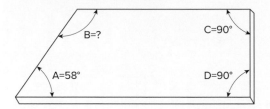

**Step 2:** Since the square-cut end produces a pair of 90° angles, the known angles of the board are 58°, 90° and 90°. Label the known angles A, C and D respectively.

**Step 3:** Apply the formula.
Angle B = 360 − (Angle A + Angle C + Angle D)
Angle B = 360 − (58 + 90 + 90)
Angle B = 360 − 238
Angle B = 122°

**BASIC WOODSHOP GEOMETRY** *Part Two*

*Part Three*

# USING MATH
# IN THE WOODSHOP

CHAPTER 11

# *Enlarging Grid Patterns*

Unlike an arc, which has a constant radius, an irregular curve (as defined in chapter six) is a curve with a constantly changing radius. Woodworking projects often include parts with irregular curves. Such curves add interesting shapes to parts like bracket feet, table legs, aprons, stretchers, decorative scrollwork designs, toy parts and more.

However, when working from a plan in a woodworking book or magazine, project parts with irregular curves can be a bit problematic. Because books and magazines are relatively small in size, full-size curved parts can't usually be shown. Also, irregular curves can't be accurately defined using the length, width and depth dimensions used to detail the size and shape of most parts.

To solve this problem, books and magazines usually add a grid pattern to irregularly curved parts. A grid pattern allows book and magazine editors to present irregular curves in a reduced size, yet the grid provides all the information needed for the reader to enlarge the curve to full size.

Short of buying a pantograph, a grid pattern can be enlarged to full size in a couple of ways. The *grid square method* is the one most commonly used, although, as photocopiers become more common, the *photocopy method* is gaining favor with many woodworkers. This chapter shows you how to do both.

## The Grid Square Method

Many woodworkers quickly become glassy-eyed when faced with using the grid square method to enlarge a pattern. Perhaps it's a suspicion that one must be blessed with artistic talent in order to do an enlargement. Believe me—and this comes from someone who has trouble drawing straight lines with a good ruler—nothing can be further from the truth. This procedure is pretty straightforward, and once you understand it, you'll no longer find yourself squaring the corners of a gracefully curved bracket foot in order to avoid the procedure altogether.

Let's look at an example and work through it step by step.

**Step 1:** Determine the grid scale.
Locate the scale, which can usually be found in an area adjacent to the grid pattern. Commonly used scales are: 1 square = ½", 1 square = ¾", 1 square = 1" (the most common scale); 1 square = 1½" and 1 square = 2". Our example uses a scale of 1 square = 1".

USING MATH IN THE WOODSHOP

*Part Three*

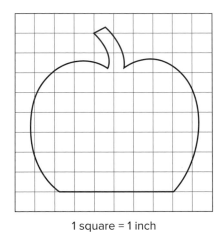

1 square = 1 inch

**Step 3:** Lay out a full-size grid.
On a clean piece of paper, use a ruler to scribe horizontal and vertical lines corresponding to the number of lines used on the grid pattern. The distance between each line is determined by the grid scale: 1" in our example.

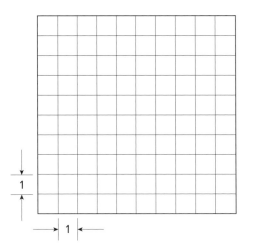

**Step 2:** Number the squares on the grid pattern. Working from a common corner, number each of the grid lines in both a horizontal and vertical direction.

1 square = 1 inch

*Part Three*
**USING MATH IN THE WOODSHOP**

**Step 4:** Number the lines on the full-size grid. Working from the same common corner established in step 2, number the horizontal and vertical lines to correspond with those on the grid pattern.

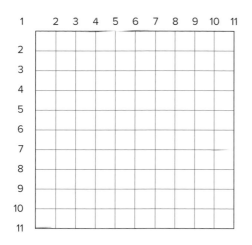

**Step 5:** Mark the corresponding points of intersection.

Looking at the grid pattern, note where the curved pattern intersects with a grid line. Find the corresponding point of intersection on the full-size grid and mark that point with a dot. Continue this procedure, adding dots at each corresponding point of intersection between the curved pattern and the grid lines. The numbered lines, which serve as guides, will help minimize confusion. When completed, the full-size grid will look much like a connect-the-dots pattern.

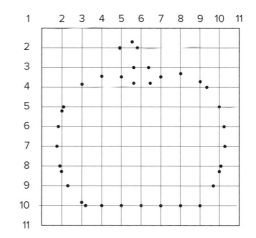

USING MATH IN THE WOODSHOP

*Part Three*

**Step 6:** Connect the dots.

With the dots as a guide, you should be able to make a freehand sketch that's pretty close to the one on the grid pattern. If this isn't working to your satisfaction, use a french curve or a flexible curve to help with the job. Both of these drawing tools are sold at most art supply stores. Keep in mind that, in most cases, the full-size grid pattern doesn't have to be a perfect copy of the original pattern, so don't worry too much if the match isn't exact.

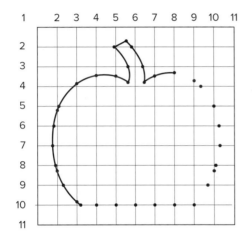

## The Photocopy Method

A photocopier can be a real time-saver when enlarging a pattern. Not only does the photocopier save time, you'll find that a pattern doesn't even require a grid in order to be enlarged—you simply work from the curved pattern as shown in the book or magazine.

The table shown here requires the use of a photocopier that can enlarge at least 150 percent. To find such a machine, check your local copy center. The enlargements are accurate to within 1 percent.

You'll need to determine the percentage of enlargement before you can use the table. To determine the percentage of enlargement:

1.  Determine the desired full-size length of the pattern for the finished project.
2.  Measure the length of the pattern in the book.
3.  Divide the desired full-size length by the measured length of the pattern in the book, then multiply by 100.

**EXAMPLE:**

Plans for a hutch cupboard show a grid pattern for a curved bracket foot. The full-size curve must measure 6" long. On the pattern, the curve measured 1⅞" inches long. How much must the curve be enlarged to produce a full-size pattern?

Percentage of enlargement =

$$\frac{\text{Desired full-size length}}{\text{Measured length of pattern on grid}} \times 100$$

$$= \frac{6}{1\frac{7}{8}} \times 100$$

$$= 3.2 \times 100$$

$$= 320 \text{ percent}$$

Once the percentage of enlargement is known, the table on the next page details how to enlarge the pattern using a photocopier.

*Part Three*
**USING MATH IN THE WOODSHOP**

| To enlarge original by: (% of enlargement) | Step 1 Photocopy original using a setting % of: | Step 2 Photocopy first copy using a setting % of: | Step 3 Photocopy second copy using a setting % of: | Step 4 Photocopy third copy using a setting % of: |
|---|---|---|---|---|
| 155 | 150 | 103 | - | - |
| 160 | 150 | 107 | - | - |
| 165 | 150 | 110 | - | - |
| 170 | 150 | 113 | - | - |
| 175 | 150 | 117 | - | - |
| 180 | 150 | 120 | - | - |
| 185 | 150 | 123 | - | - |
| 190 | 150 | 127 | - | - |
| 195 | 150 | 130 | - | - |
| 200 | 150 | 133 | - | - |
| 205 | 150 | 137 | - | - |
| 210 | 150 | 140 | - | - |
| 215 | 150 | 143 | - | - |
| 220 | 150 | 147 | - | - |
| 225 | 150 | 150 | - | - |
| 230 | 150 | 150 | 102 | - |
| 235 | 150 | 150 | 104 | - |
| 240 | 150 | 150 | 107 | - |
| 245 | 150 | 150 | 109 | - |
| 250 | 150 | 150 | 111 | - |
| 255 | 150 | 150 | 113 | - |
| 260 | 150 | 150 | 116 | - |
| 265 | 150 | 150 | 118 | - |
| 270 | 150 | 150 | 120 | - |
| 275 | 150 | 150 | 122 | - |

*Part Three* **USING MATH IN THE WOODSHOP**

| To enlarge original by: (% of enlargement) | Step 1 Photocopy original using a setting % of: | Step 2 Photocopy first copy using a setting % of: | Step 3 Photocopy second copy using a setting % of: | Step 4 Photocopy third copy using a setting % of: |
|---|---|---|---|---|
| 280 | 150 | 150 | 124 | - |
| 285 | 150 | 150 | 127 | - |
| 290 | 150 | 150 | 129 | - |
| 295 | 150 | 150 | 131 | - |
| 300 | 150 | 150 | 133 | - |
| 305 | 150 | 150 | 136 | - |
| 310 | 150 | 150 | 138 | - |
| 315 | 150 | 150 | 140 | - |
| 320 | 150 | 150 | 142 | - |
| 325 | 150 | 150 | 144 | - |
| 330 | 150 | 150 | 147 | - |
| 335 | 150 | 150 | 149 | - |
| 340 | 150 | 150 | 150 | 101 |
| 345 | 150 | 150 | 150 | 102 |
| 350 | 150 | 150 | 150 | 104 |
| 355 | 150 | 150 | 150 | 105 |
| 360 | 150 | 150 | 150 | 107 |
| 365 | 150 | 150 | 150 | 108 |
| 370 | 150 | 150 | 148 | 111 |
| 375 | 150 | 150 | 150 | 111 |
| 380 | 150 | 150 | 148 | 114 |
| 385 | 150 | 150 | 150 | 114 |
| 390 | 150 | 150 | 148 | 117 |
| 395 | 150 | 150 | 150 | 117 |
| 400 | 150 | 150 | 148 | 120 |

*Part Three*
USING MATH IN THE WOODSHOP

CHAPTER 12

# Simplifying Compound Angles

A *compound angle* is created when a workpiece is cut at an angle using a saw blade that is also tilted at an angle (Fig. 12-1). The compound angle is commonly used to create taper-sided boxes and containers. The tilt angle of the box side is measured from a vertical line (Fig. 12-2). Compound angles can be cut on the table saw or the radial-arm saw. Keep in mind, however, that saw gauges are notoriously inaccurate, so it's always best to make test cuts on scrap stock.

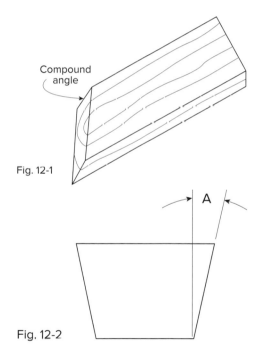

Compound angle

Fig. 12-1

Fig. 12-2

The saw blade angle (B) is measured from a vertical line for both the table saw and radial-arm saw (Fig. 12-3). The angle of the table saw miter gauge is measured from a line perpendicular to the saw blade (Fig. 12-4). The angle of the radial-arm saw is measured from a line perpendicular to the fence (Fig. 12-5).

Not all manufacturers use the same points of reference when establishing the blade tilt and cutting angles shown on their saw gauges. Therefore, the angles marked on your saw gauge might not correspond with the angles shown in the table. To avoid confusion, always set the saw based on angles B and C in Figures 12-3, 12-4 and 12-5.

A = tilt angle of sides
B = blade angle of table saw or radial-arm saw
C = angle of table saw miter gauge or radial-arm saw

USING MATH IN THE WOODSHOP

*Part Three*

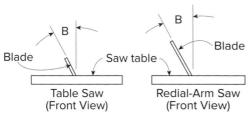

Fig. 12-3

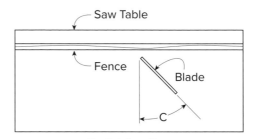

Redial-Arm Saw
(Front View)

Fig. 12-5

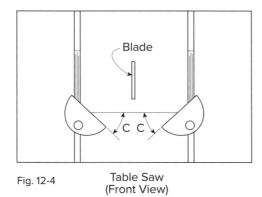

Fig. 12-4

Table Saw
(Front View)

| Four-Sided Figure | A (Degrees) Fig. 12-2 | B (Degrees) Fig. 12-3 | C (Degrees) Fig. 12-4 & 12-5 |
|---|---|---|---|
| | 5 | 44.8 | 4.9 |
| | 10 | 44.1 | 9.9 |
| | 15 | 43.1 | 14.5 |
| | 20 | 41.6 | 18.9 |
| | 25 | 39.9 | 22.9 |
| | 30 | 37.8 | 26.6 |
| | 35 | 35.4 | 29.8 |
| | 40 | 32.8 | 32.7 |
| | 45 | 30.0 | 35.3 |
| | 50 | 27.0 | 37.5 |
| | 55 | 23.9 | 39.3 |
| | 60 | 20.7 | 40.9 |
| **Five-Sided Figure** | **A (Degrees)** | **B (Degrees)** | **C (Degrees)** |
| | 5 | 35.8 | 3.6 |
| | 10 | 35.4 | 7.2 |
| | 15 | 34.6 | 10.7 |
| | 20 | 33.6 | 14.0 |
| | 25 | 32.2 | 17.1 |
| | 30 | 30.6 | 20.0 |
| | 35 | 28.8 | 22.6 |
| | 40 | 26.8 | 25.0 |
| | 45 | 24.6 | 27.2 |
| | 50 | 22.2 | 29.1 |
| | 55 | 19.7 | 30.8 |
| | 60 | 17.1 | 32.2 |

| Six-Sided Figure | A (Degrees) | B (Degrees) | C (Degrees) |
|---|---|---|---|
| | 5 | 29.9 | 2.9 |
| | 10 | 29.5 | 5.7 |
| | 15 | 28.9 | 8.5 |
| | 20 | 28.0 | 11.2 |
| | 25 | 27.0 | 13.7 |
| | 30 | 25.7 | 16.1 |
| | 35 | 24.2 | 18.3 |
| | 40 | 22.5 | 20.4 |
| | 45 | 20.7 | 22.2 |
| | 50 | 18.8 | 23.9 |
| | 55 | 16.7 | 25.3 |
| | 60 | 14.5 | 26.6 |
| **Eight-Sided Figure** | **A (Degrees)** | **B (Degrees)** | **C (Degrees)** |
| | 5 | 22.4 | 2.1 |
| | 10 | 22.1 | 4.1 |
| | 15 | 21.7 | 6.1 |
| | 20 | 21.1 | 8.1 |
| | 25 | 20.3 | 9.9 |
| | 30 | 19.4 | 11.7 |
| | 35 | 18.3 | 13.4 |
| | 40 | 17.1 | 14.9 |
| | 45 | 15.7 | 16.3 |
| | 50 | 14.2 | 17.6 |
| | 55 | 12.7 | 18.7 |
| | 60 | 11.0 | 19.7 |

| Ten-Sided Figure | A (Degrees) | B (Degrees) | C (Degrees) |
|---|---|---|---|
| | 5 | 17.9 | 1.6 |
| | 10 | 17.7 | 3.2 |
| | 15 | 17.4 | 4.8 |
| | 20 | 16.9 | 6.3 |
| | 25 | 16.3 | 7.8 |
| | 30 | 15.5 | 9.2 |
| | 35 | 14.7 | 10.6 |
| | 40 | 13.7 | 11.8 |
| | 45 | 12.6 | 12.9 |
| | 50 | 11.5 | 14.0 |
| | 55 | 10.2 | 14.9 |
| | 60 | 8.9 | 15.7 |
| Twelve-Sided Figure | A (Degrees) | B (Degrees) | C (Degrees) |
| | 5 | 14.9 | 1.3 |
| | 10 | 14.8 | 2.7 |
| | 15 | 14.5 | 4.0 |
| | 20 | 14.1 | 5.2 |
| | 25 | 13.6 | 6.5 |
| | 30 | 13.0 | 7.6 |
| | 35 | 12.2 | 8.7 |
| | 40 | 11.4 | 9.8 |
| | 45 | 10.6 | 10.7 |
| | 50 | 9.6 | 11.6 |
| | 55 | 8.5 | 12.4 |
| | 60 | 7.4 | 13.1 |

**WOODSHOP APPLICATION**

## *Cutting Compound Angles*

Using your table saw, you want to build a four-sided flatware tray that has a tilt angle of 20°. What table saw settings are going to produce the correct compound miter angle?

**Step 1:** Find the table for four-sided figures.

**Step 2:** Find the row for a tilt angle (A) of 20°.

**Step 3:** Read across the row to find a table saw blade angle (B) of 41.6° and a miter gauge angle (C) of 18.9°.

CHAPTER 13

# Solving Right Triangles

From chapter six, you will recall that a *right triangle* has one 90° angle (Fig. 13-1). Right triangles are found in many woodworking designs. For example, a miter becomes a right triangle simply by scribing a line perpendicular to the edge of the board (Fig. 13-2), as does a dovetail (Fig. 13-3). The back of an early American hooded cradle includes four right triangles (Fig. 13-4).

A right triangle has a *hypotenuse,* a fancy word meaning the side opposite the right angle. The hypotenuse is always the longest side of the triangle. The remaining two sides of the triangle are called the *legs.* Sometimes the horizontal leg is called the *base,* and the vertical leg is called the *side.* The intersection of the two legs forms the right angle. In most drawings of a right triangle, a small box is added to designate that the angle shown is a right angle.

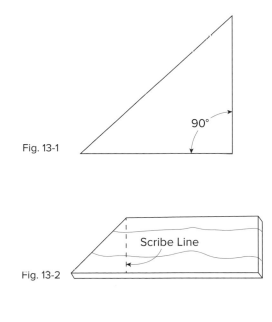

Fig. 13-1

90°

Scribe Line

Fig. 13-2

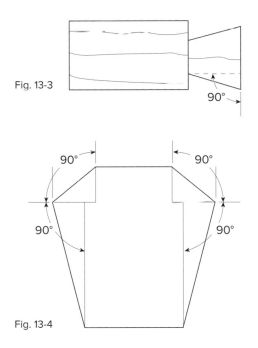

Fig. 13-3

90°

90°        90°

90°        90°

Fig. 13-4

USING MATH IN THE WOODSHOP

*Part Three*

Because we encounter right triangles with such regularity in the woodshop, it's useful to be able to calculate the lengths of the triangle sides and the angles they form. The process of doing these calculations is commonly referred to as *solving a right triangle*. Once you can solve right triangles, you'll be surprised how often you use the skill in the woodshop.

This chapter shows how to solve right triangles using either the *Pythagorean theorem method* or the *table method*. The Pythagorean theorem method detailed here enables you to determine the side lengths of a right triangle, while the table method shows how to determine not only the side lengths, but also the angles of a right triangle.

## Using the Pythagorean Theorem

Pythagoras, a Greek philosopher, teacher and mathematician who lived around 500 BC, is credited with proving that there is a proportional relationship between the sides of a right triangle. His theorem, which we now call the Pythagorean theorem, states that in any right triangle, the square of the hypotenuse is equal to the sum of the squares of the two other sides. Basically, this means that if you know the length of any two sides of a right triangle, you can determine the third side. Written as a formula, it looks like this:

$A^2 + B^2 = C^2$
A = the base
B = the side
C = the hypotenuse

The same formula can be written in several other useful forms:

$A = \sqrt{C^2 - B^2}$

$B = \sqrt{C^2 - A^2}$

$C = \sqrt{A^2 + B^2}$

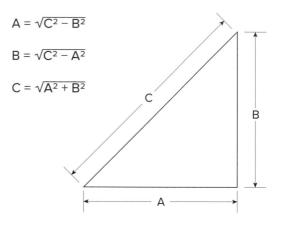

Fig. 13-5

*Part Three*

**USING MATH IN THE WOODSHOP**

WOODSHOP APPLICATION

# *Using the Pythagorean Theorem to Solve a Right Triangle*
## *(Solving for One Side When Two Sides Are Known)*

Suppose you need to cut a right-angled gusset to serve as a stiffener for the back of a case (Fig. 13-6). To fit in the available space, the gusset must measure 5" diagonally and have a base that's 4" long. What is the length of the remaining side?

**Step 1:** Determine what is known about the right triangle. As shown in Fig. 13-6, you know the following:
A = the base = 4"
B = the side = unknown
C = the hypotenuse = 5"

**Step 2:** Determine if the known information allows you to solve the triangle. You know the length of two sides of the right triangle (A and C), therefore you can solve for the unknown side (B).

**Step 3:** Select the equation that allows you to solve the unknown. Use the equation that solves for B.

$$B = \sqrt{C^2 - A^2}$$

**Step 4:** Solve the equation.

$$B = \sqrt{5^2 - 4^2}$$

$$B = \sqrt{25 - 16}$$

$$B = \sqrt{9}$$

$$B = 3$$

The side is 3" long.

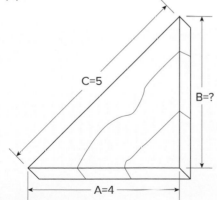

Fig. 13-6

## Using Tables

Using the formulas that follow, you can determine the unknown sides of a right triangle if you know one of the angles (other than the 90° angle) and the length of one side. You can also determine the unknown angles of a right triangle if you know the lengths of at least two of the sides.

In some cases it might be necessary to use two of the formulas to get the answer you need. The first formula solves for an unknown side or angle. Then, the new information is applied to a second formula that can provide the final answer. Of course, if you know two of the sides and want to know the third, you can also use the Pythagorean theorem as discussed earlier. However, when using tables, note that the triangles are labeled differently than when using the Pythagorean theorem.

The reference angle (A) is the angle (other than the 90° angle) used to help solve the triangle (Fig. 13-7). It is important to keep in mind that when the location of the reference angle changes, the locations of sides B and C also change.

Finally, remember that the three angles in a triangle always equal 180°. If you know one of the angles (other than the 90° angle) you can get the unknown angle using the following formula.

Unknown Angle = 180 − (90 + known angle).

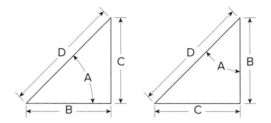

Fig. 13-7

A = reference angle (based on Angle Functions in tables I, II or III)
B = side adjacent to the reference angle
C = side opposite the reference angle
D = side opposite the 90° angle (the hypotenuse)

*Part Three*
**USING MATH IN THE WOODSHOP**

## Angle Functions

| Angle (A) (In Degrees) | Tables | | |
|---|---|---|---|
| | I | II | III |
| 0 | .00000 | 1.00000 | .00000 |
| 1 | .01746 | .99985 | .01745 |
| 2 | .03492 | .99939 | .03490 |
| 3 | .05241 | .99863 | .05234 |
| 4 | .06993 | .99756 | .06976 |
| 5 | .08749 | .99619 | .08716 |
| 6 | .10510 | .99452 | .10453 |
| 7 | .12278 | .99255 | .12187 |
| 8 | .14054 | .99027 | .13937 |
| 9 | .15838 | .98769 | .15643 |
| 10 | .17633 | .98481 | .17365 |
| 11 | .19438 | .98163 | .19081 |
| 12 | .21256 | .97815 | .20791 |
| 13 | .23087 | .97437 | .22495 |
| 14 | .24933 | .97030 | .24192 |
| 15 | .26795 | .96593 | .25882 |
| 16 | .28675 | .96126 | .27564 |
| 17 | .30573 | .95630 | .29237 |
| 18 | .32492 | .95106 | .30902 |
| 19 | .34433 | .94552 | .32557 |
| 20 | .36397 | .93969 | .34202 |
| 21 | .38386 | .93358 | .35837 |
| 22 | .40403 | .92718 | .37461 |
| 23 | .42447 | .92050 | .39073 |
| 24 | .44523 | .91355 | .40674 |
| 25 | .46631 | .90631 | .42262 |
| 26 | .48773 | .89879 | .43837 |

USING MATH IN THE WOODSHOP

*Part Three*

| Angle (A) (In Degrees) | Tables | | |
|:---:|:---:|:---:|:---:|
| | I | II | III |
| 27 | .50953 | .89101 | .45399 |
| 28 | .53171 | .88295 | .46947 |
| 29 | .55431 | .87462 | .48481 |
| 30 | .57735 | .86603 | .50000 |
| 31 | .60086 | .85717 | .51504 |
| 32 | .62487 | .84805 | .52992 |
| 33 | .64941 | .83867 | .54464 |
| 34 | .67451 | .82904 | .55919 |
| 35 | .70021 | .81915 | .57358 |
| 36 | .72654 | .80902 | .58779 |
| 37 | .75355 | .79864 | .60182 |
| 38 | .78129 | .78801 | .61566 |
| 39 | .80978 | .77715 | .62932 |
| 40 | .83910 | .76604 | .64279 |
| 41 | .86929 | .75471 | .65606 |
| 42 | .90040 | .74314 | .66913 |
| 43 | .93252 | .73135 | .68200 |
| 44 | .96569 | .71934 | .69466 |
| 45 | 1.00000 | .70711 | .70711 |

## Solving Right Triangles When One Side and One Angle Are Known

| If You Know the Length Of: | And You Want to Know the Length Of: | Use This Formula: |
|---|---|---|
| B | C | $C = A \text{ (from Table I)} \times B$ |
| B | D | $D = \dfrac{B}{A \text{ (from Table II)}}$ |
| C | B | $B = \dfrac{C}{A \text{ (from Table I)}}$ |
| C | D | $D = \dfrac{C}{A \text{ (from Table III)}}$ |
| D | C | $C = A \text{ (from Table III)} \times D$ |
| D | B | $B = A \text{ (from Table II)} \times D$ |

USING MATH IN THE WOODSHOP

*Part Three*

# *Using the Tables to Solve a Right Triangle*
### *(When One Side and One Angle Are Known)*

A lap desk to be built must have sides that are 14" long and have a 15° slant. If the front end of the sides measure 3", what is the overall width of the sides?

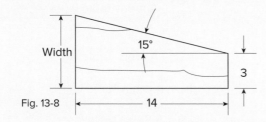

Fig. 13-8

The desk side creates a right triangle with one angle known (A) and one side known (B). To determine the overall width of a side, calculate the length of side C, then add that length to 3".

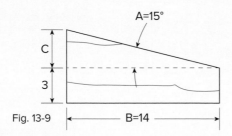

Fig. 13-9

**Step 1:** Determine what is known about the right triangle.

As shown in Fig. 13-9, you know the following:
A = the reference angle = 15°
B = the side adjacent to the reference angle = 14"
C = the side opposite the reference angle = unknown

**Step 2:** Determine if the known information allows you to solve the triangle. You know one angle (A) and the length of one side (B), therefore you can solve for the unknown side (C).

**Step 3:** Select the equation that allows you to solve for the unknown. Use the equation that solves C when you know angle A and B.
C = A (from Table I) × B

**Step 4:** Solve the equation.
Per Table I, an angle (A) of 15° has an angle function of .26795.
Therefore:
C = .26795 × 14
    = 3.7513 (round to 3.75 = 3¾")

**Step 5:** Add to determine the total width of the side.
Width of side = 3¾" + 3"
                      = 6¾"

## Solving Right Triangles When Two Sides Are Known

| If You Know the Length Of: | And You Know the Length Of: | Use This Formula: |
|---|---|---|
| B | C | A (from Table I) $= \dfrac{C}{B}$ |
| B | D | A (from Table II) $= \dfrac{B}{D}$ |
| C | D | A (from Table III) $= \dfrac{C}{D}$ |
| Once the angle function (A) is determined, use the appropriate table to find the corresponding angle. | | |

Part Three

USING MATH IN THE WOODSHOP

WOODSHOP APPLICATION

# Using the Tables to Solve a Right Triangle
## (When Two Sides Are Known)

A coffee table is to have four 15"-long legs made from 1¾" square stock. The legs are to be tapered on two sides, with each taper starting 4¼" from the top of the leg. At the bottom of the leg, the taper reduces the thickness of the leg by ¾". You need to determine the angle of the taper so that you can use a tapering jig to cut the tapers.

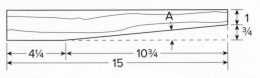

Fig. 13-10

**Step 1:** Determine what is known about the right triangle. As shown in Fig. 13-10, you know the following:
A = the reference angle = unknown
B = the side adjacent to the reference
    angle = 10¾ = 10.75
C = the side opposite the reference
    angle = ¾ = .75

**Step 2:** Determine if the known information allows you to solve the triangle. You know the length of two sides (B and C), therefore, you can solve for the unknown angle (A).

**Step 3:** Select the equation that allows you to solve the unknown. Use the equation that solves for angle A when you know sides B and C.

$$A \text{ (from Table I)} = \frac{C}{B}$$

**Step 4:** Solve the equation.

$$A \text{ (from Table I)} = \frac{C}{B}$$

$$= \frac{.75}{10.75}$$

$$= 0.06977$$

**From Table I:** An angle function of 0.06977 equals an angle of about 4°. Therefore, the angle of the taper (A) is 4°.

CHAPTER 14

# *Applying Handy Woodshop Formulas*

An *equation* shows that two numbers or two groups of numbers equal the same amount. A *formula,* on the other hand, is an equation that shows a unique relationship between certain things. For example, when working with a triangular part, we know that the formula $A = \frac{1}{2}B \times H$ shows the unique relationship between certain things in a triangle, specifically the area (A), length of the base (B) and the height (H).

I prefer to define a formula in simpler terms. To me, a formula is simply a concise set of instructions for solving a particular problem. Indeed, a good formula, properly applied, can take a tough task and reduce it to a simple exercise in basic arithmetic.

This chapter provides a smorgasbord of easy-to-use formulas for use in the woodshop. Once you learn how to apply the formulas, you'll be able to solve an assortment of problems—from figuring the moisture content of wood to calculating the weight of a cherry tabletop.

## Determining Wood Moisture Content

A moisture meter is the fastest and easiest way to measure the moisture content in a piece of wood. Although moisture meters have become more affordable in recent years, most woodworkers don't own one.

Without a moisture meter in hand, your other option is to calculate the moisture content of the wood. Although the procedure is very accurate, it isn't altogether practical for the average hobbyist woodworker. That's because you need a laboratory (gram) scale or an equivalent scale to get accurate weight measurements of the wood sample. Then, too, it can take up to 24 hours for the wood sample to fully dry in a kitchen oven—a procedure that's likely to disrupt any cooking schedule.

If, despite the drawbacks, you are still inclined to do this calculation, you'll need a wood sample that's about 1" thick by 3" wide by 1" long (Fig. 14-1). Cutting the sample in this manner exposes a considerable amount of end grain, which helps the sample dry faster. Check to make sure that the sample doesn't have any knots or other defects. Also, avoid cutting the sample from the ends, which tend to be drier than other parts of the board.

Using the laboratory scale, weigh the sample and note the weight. Then place the sample in the oven and bake it at a temperature of 210° to 220° Fahrenheit. Reweigh the sample about every eight hours, taking care to avoid scorching the wood as it dries. When the sample no longer loses weight it is at the oven-dry weight, which means it is completely free of water and has a moisture content of zero. Once you have the oven-dry weight of the sample, you can determine the wood moisture content (MC) by using the following formula:

$$MC = \frac{\text{Original Weight} - \text{Oven-Dry Weight}}{\text{Oven Dry Weight}} \times 100$$

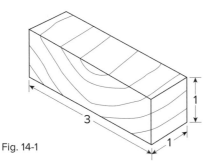

Fig. 14-1

## Determining Side Lengths for Polygons

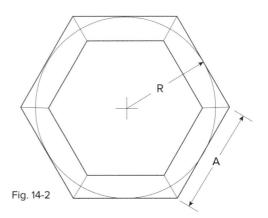

Fig. 14-2

WOODSHOP APPLICATION

# *Determining Wood Moisture Content*

The original weight of a sample is 14 grams. After completely drying in the oven, the sample weighs 12 grams. What is the moisture content of the sample?

$$MC = \frac{\text{Original Weight} - \text{Oven-Dry Weight}}{\text{Oven-Dry Weight}} \times 100$$

$$= \frac{14 \text{ grams} - 12 \text{ grams}}{12 \text{ grams}} \times 100$$

$$= \frac{2 \text{ grams}}{12 \text{ grams}} \times 100$$

$$= .167 \times 100$$

$$= 16.7 \text{ percent}$$

For any figure with sides of equal length, use the following formula to calculate the lengths of the sides:

$A = R \times C$

$A$ = length of side

$C$ = constant (see Constant Chart below)

$R$ = radius of a circle that is tangent to the sides of the polygon

### Constant Chart

| Number of Equal-Length Sides | Constant |
|---|---|
| 3 (equilateral triangle) | 3.464 |
| 4 (square) | 2.000 |
| 5 (regular pentagon) | 1.453 |
| 6 (regular hexagon) | 1.155 |
| 8 (regular octagon) | 0.828 |
| 10 (regular decagon) | 0.650 |
| 12 (regular dodecagon) | 0.536 |

*Part Three*

**USING MATH IN THE WOODSHOP**

WOODSHOP APPLICATION

## *Determining Side Lengths for a Polygon*

You are preparing to build an octagonal wall clock that must be 16" wide. What length do you cut each of the eight sides?

A 16"-wide clock has a radius of 8".
The constant for a regular octagon is 0.828.
$A = R \times C$
$\quad = 8 \times .0828$
$\quad = 6.624"$ (round to 6⅝")
Cut each side to a length of 6⅝".

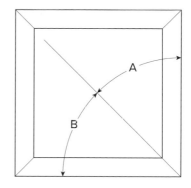

Square (also Rectangle)
$A = 45°$
$B = 45°$

## Miter Angles for Polygons (When All Sides Are Equal Length)

The miter angles for several common polygons are shown. For polygons not shown, use the miter angle formula that follows to calculate the angle.

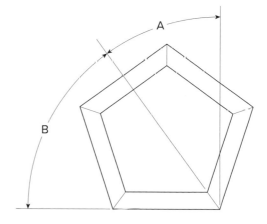

Regular Pentagon
$A = 36°$
$B = 54°$

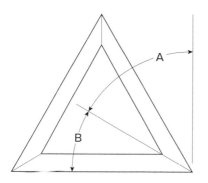

Equilateral Triangle
$A = 60°$
$B = 30°$

Part Three
USING MATH IN THE WOODSHOP

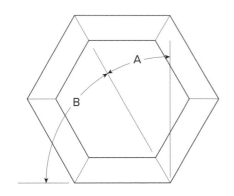

Regular Hexagon
A = 30°
B = 60°

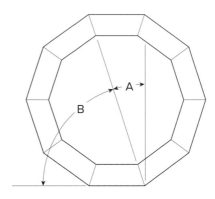

Regular Decagon
A = 18°
B = 72°

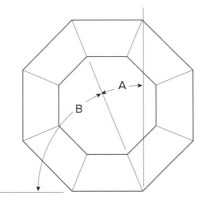

Regular Octagon
A = 22½°
B = 67½°

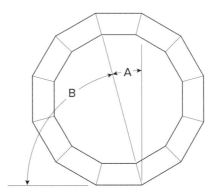

Regular Dodecagon
A = 15°
B = 75°

*Part Three*
**USING MATH IN THE WOODSHOP**

## Miter Angle Formula

For any figure with sides of equal length, use the following formula to calculate the miter angle (A):

$$A = \frac{180°}{N}$$

A = the miter angle (measured from vertical)
N = the number of sides

**WOODSHOP APPLICATION**

### Using the Miter Angle Formula

You are building a box with nine equal sides. What is the miter angle for each of the sides?

$$A = \frac{180°}{N}$$

$$A = \frac{180°}{9}$$

$$A = 20°$$

## Arc Formulas

Use these formulas to calculate the dimensions of an arc.

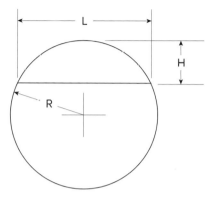

$$L = 2\sqrt{H\,(2R - H)}$$

$$R = \frac{L^2 + 4H^2}{8H}$$

$$H = R - \left(\frac{\sqrt{4R^2 - L^2}}{2}\right)$$

where:
L = the arc length
H = the arc height
R = the arc radius

USING MATH IN THE WOODSHOP

*Part Three*

WOODSHOP APPLICATION

## Using the Arc Formulas

The ends of a bench require an arc-shaped cutout that measures 3" high and 12" long. What is the radius (R) of the arc?

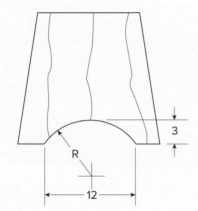

**Step 1:** Since the height and length of the arc are known, you can use the formula that solves for the arc radius.

$$R = \frac{L^2 + 4H^2}{8H}$$

**Step 2:** Plug in the knowns and solve the formula.

$$R = \frac{12^2 + (4 \times 3^2)}{(8 \times 3)}$$

$$R = \frac{144 + 36}{24}$$

$$R = \frac{180}{24}$$

$$R = 7.5$$

The arc has a radius of 7½".

## Calculating Shelf Deflection

### How to Make Sure Shelves Don't Sag Too Much

We ask our wood shelves to do a lot of work. We fill them with books and magazines that can weigh 40 pounds per foot or more. We put sewing machines on them, heavy laundry baskets, stacks of canned goods, and anything else we can squeeze on them.

Add enough weight to a shelf and it will surely bend near the midpoint. The more weight that's added, the more the board bends. Wood technologists use the term *deflection* to describe such a bend. Most everyone else simply calls it *sag*.

A well-designed shelf should be strong enough to minimize sag to the point that it won't be noticed. Our eyes won't see sag if it's less than ⅟₃₂" (0.0313") per foot of shelf length.

Be aware, though, as time passes, a constant weight on a shelf can cause the initial sag to increase by up to 50 percent. To account for that future-sag, called *creep,* the initial deflection of a shelf should not be more than 0.021" per foot. That way, if creep sets in, the sag won't ever go beyond the 1/32" per foot limit.

Shelf sag can be approximately calculated using the two formulas shown here. The first one gets you the maximum sag at the mid-point of the shelf. The second formula converts the maximum sag at the mid-point to sag in inches per foot. Once you have the inches-per-foot number, you can compare it to the limit of 0.021 in. per foot.

Before you can use the first formula, you'll need to determine a few things: the thickness, width and length of the shelf; the total amount of weight on the shelf; the wood species; and, from the chart, the Strength Value for the wood species. Use "actual" (measured) dimensions for thickness and length, not "nominal" dimensions. That means, if you buy a 1 x 12 (nominal size) ponderosa pine board at a lumberyard, plug its actual dimensions (¾" thick by 11-¼" wide) into the formula.

The formula is based on laboratory tests done on optimal-quality wood, meaning it's dry, straight-grained, and defect-free. Most of us aren't going to have perfectly straight-grained and totally defect-free wood at our disposal, so the actual sag is likely to be at least slightly more than the calculated number. Boards with big knots should be avoided as their strength values will be well below the norm for the species. Indeed, in a worst case, a board with a big knot could snap in two when weight is added.

The first formula assumes that all the weight is concentrated at the midpoint of the shelf. Were that same weight distributed across the full length of the shelf, it would produce slightly less sag.

The advantage of using a formula based on a mid-point-concentrated weight is that you get a built-in safety factor.

Also, keep in mind that the formula assumes the ends of the shelf are not fixed in place. Shelves with fixed-in-place ends are better able to resist sag. So, if your shelf-ends are fixed, the actual sag should be less than the calculated sag.

One last point here. The Strength Value (F) shown in the chart is based on something engineers call the *modulus of elasticity* or *MOE.* The MOE for any given material, wood included, is a measure of the stiffness of a material. To put it another way, it's a measure of how well a material resists bending.

The MOE is always a very large number. For example, the MOE of black walnut is 1,680,000, typically written as $1.68 \times 10^6$. The MOE of yellow poplar is 1,580,000 or $1.58 \times 10^6$.

To simplify the equation used here, the MOE is shortened by removing the last two digits and rewritten as a *strength value.* The Strength Value chart includes most common wood species, but not all of them.

If the wood species you are using isn't included in the chart, you'll need to find its MOE and convert it to a strength value by removing the last two digits. You can find the MOE for many wood species in various engineering manuals, including the *Wood Handbook* published by the U.S. Forest Products Laboratory (online at www.fpl.fs.fed.us).

All that said, if you want to avoid doing any of the math, I suggest you take a look at a website called "The Sagulator" (www.woodbin.com/calcs/sagulator). It's excellent, and a dirt-simple way to determine sag. Just plug in the numbers to instantly get mid-point sag and sag per foot.

*Part Three* **USING MATH IN THE WOODSHOP**

## Formula for Determining Deflection (Sag) at Midpoint of Shelf Length

$$A = \frac{(B^3)\,(C)}{(D^3)\,(E)\,(F)\,(400)}$$ where:

A = deflection at center of shelf (in inches)
B = length of shelf (in inches)
C = weight of contents (in pounds)
D = thickness of shelf (in inches)
E = width of shelf (in inches)
F = strength value (from chart)

### EXAMPLE:

You're installing a black walnut shelf that measures ⅞" (0.875") thick by 8" wide by 34" long. The shelf will be filled with glass dishes and the total weight of all the dishes is 50 pounds. How much will the shelf deflect at its mid-point when the glass is added?

**Step 1:** Write the formula:

$$A = \frac{(B^3)\,(C)}{(D^3)\,(E)\,(F)\,(400)}$$

**Step 2:** Determine the knowns:
B = 34"
C = 50 pounds
D = 0.875"
E = 8"
F (from chart, for black walnut) = 16,800

**Step 3:** Plug in the knowns and solve the formula.

$$A = \frac{(34^3)\,(50)}{(0.875^3)\,(8)\,(16,800)\,(400)}$$

$$A = \frac{(39,304)\,(50)}{(0.670)\,(8)\,(16,800)\,(400)}$$

$$A = \frac{1,965,200}{36,019,200}$$

A = **0.055"**

So the shelf deflects 0.055" (slightly less than ⅟₁₆") at its midpoint when the 50 pounds of dishes are added.

To determine how much that same shelf deflects per foot of length, use this formula:

$$DPF = \frac{(12)\,(A)}{B}$$ where:

DPF = deflection per foot of shelf length
A = deflection at center of shelf (from formula)
B = shelf length (in inches)

$$DPF = \frac{(12)\,(0.055)}{34}$$

$$DPF = \frac{0.660}{34}$$

**DPF = 0.019" per foot**

The shelf deflects 0.019" for every foot of shelf length.

As mentioned earlier, because our eyes won't notice any deflection less than 0.021" for every foot of shelf length, the deflection for this shelf is acceptable.

## Strength Value Chart

| Wood Species | Strength Value |
|---|---|
| Alder (Red) | 13,800 |
| Ash (Black) | 16,000 |
| Ash (White) | 17,400 |
| Aspen (Quaking) | 11,800 |
| Basswood (American) | 14,600 |
| Beech (American) | 17,200 |
| Birch (Yellow) | 20,100 |
| Butternut | 11,800 |
| Cedar (Western Red) | 11,100 |
| Cherry (Black) | 14,900 |
| Chestnut | 12,300 |
| Fir (Balsam) | 14,500 |
| Hickory (Shagbark) | 21,600 |
| Ipe | 31,400 |
| Mahogany | 14,000 |
| Maple (Red) | 16,400 |
| Maple (Sugar) | 18,300 |
| Oak (Red) | 18,200 |
| Oak (White) | 17,800 |
| Pine (Eastern White) | 12,400 |

| Wood Species | Strength Value |
|---|---|
| Pine (Longleaf) | 19,800 |
| Pine (Ponderosa) | 12,900 |
| Pine (Red) | 16,300 |
| Pine (Shortleaf) | 17,500 |
| Pine (Sugar) | 11,900 |
| Poplar (Yellow) | 15,800 |
| Redwood | 11,000 |
| Rosewood (Brazilian) | 18,800 |
| Spruce (Sitka) | 15,700 |
| Sweetgum | 16,400 |
| Sycamore | 14,200 |
| Teak | 15,500 |
| Walnut (Black) | 16,800 |
| **Other Materials** | **Strength Value** |
| MDF (Interior, Grade HD) | 5000 |
| MDF (Interior, Grade MD) | 3500 |
| MDF (Interior, Grade LD) | 2000 |
| Particleboard (Grade H-1) | 3481 |
| Particleboard (Grade H-2) | 3481 |
| Particleboard (Grade H-3) | 3989 |
| Particleboard (Grade M-1) | 2502 |
| Particleboard (Grade M-S) | 2756 |
| Particleboard (Grade M-2) | 3263 |
| Particleboard (Grade M-3) | 3989 |
| Particleboard (Grade LD-1) | 798 |
| Particleboard (Grade LD-2) | 1487 |

## Calculating Concentrated Load on a Particleboard Shelf

You want to place a 60-pound workshop dehumidifier by itself in the center of a ¾" thick by 10" wide by 36" long grade M-2 particleboard shelf. Can the shelf support the concentrated load?

**Step 1:** Calculate concentrated load safety factor.

Concentrated load safety factor =

$$\frac{\text{expected load on shelf (in pounds)}}{.625}$$

$$= \frac{60 \text{ pounds}}{.625}$$

$$= 96 \text{ pounds}$$

**Step 2:** Calculate the area of the shelf (in square feet).

Area of shelf = shelf width × shelf length

$$= 10" \times 36"$$

$$= 360 \text{ square inches}$$

Convert square inches to square feet (see conversion table in appendix).

Area of shelf = 360 square inches × .00694 = 2.5 square feet

**Step 3:** Calculate the uniform load.

Uniform load =

$$\frac{\text{expected load on the shelf (in pounds)}}{\text{area of shelf (in square feet)}}$$

$$= \frac{96 \text{ pounds}}{2.5 \text{ square feet}}$$

$$= 38.4 \text{ psf}$$

As shown in the chart, ¾" thick by 36" long shelf can support a uniform load of only 10 pounds per square foot. However, 1⅛"-thick particleboard can support 45 pounds per square foot. Replace ¾"-thick particleboard with 1⅛"-thick particleboard.

## Maximum Loads for Particleboard Shelving
### (For Uniformly Loaded Grade M-2 Particleboard)

| Shelf Span (Inches) | Maximum Deflection (Inches) | Uniform Load (Pounds per Sq. Ft.) | | | | |
|---|---|---|---|---|---|---|
| | | Shelf thickness (inches) | | | | |
| | | ½ | ⅝ | ¾ | 1 | 1⅛ |
| 16 | .089 | 45 | 95 | 124 | 166 | 186 |
| 20 | .111 | 20 | 45 | 80 | 130 | 146 |
| 24 | .133 | 13 | 25 | 45 | 107 | 120 |
| 28 | .156 | 8 | 15 | 25 | 70 | 100 |
| 32 | .178 | — | 10 | 18 | 45 | 65 |
| 36 | .200 | — | 5 | 10 | 30 | 45 |
| 40 | .222 | — | — | 8 | 20 | 30 |
| 44 | .244 | — | — | 5 | 15 | 25 |
| 48 | .267 | — | — | — | 10 | 15 |
| 52 | .289 | — | — | — | 8 | 10 |
| 56 | .311 | — | — | — | 5 | 8 |
| 60 | .333 | — | — | — | — | 5 |

Chart courtesy the National Particleboard Association.

Part Three
USING MATH IN THE WOODSHOP

## Determining Bandsaw Blade Length

Suppose it's time to replace your bandsaw blade, but you can't remember the blade length, and to make matters worse, you can't find the owner's manual. No need to despair; this formula will provide you with the correct length in short order.

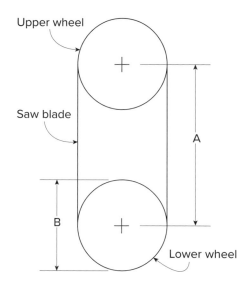

L = (2 × A) + (3.14 × B)
where:
L = bandsaw blade length (in inches)
A = distance between the bandsaw wheel center lines (in inches)
B = diameter of either the upper or lower wheel (in inches)
Note: Formula applies only to bandsaws that operate using a pair of same-sized wheels. Also, before measuring the A dimension, locate the adjustable upper (tension) wheel so it is midway between the fully up and fully down positions.

WOODSHOP APPLICATION

## *Determining the Length of a Bandsaw Blade*

You've purchased a used bandsaw at a garage sale, but the blade and owner's manual are missing. What's the correct blade length to buy?

**Step 1:** Measure the distance between the bandsaw wheel center lines (in inches). Let's say it measures 20", therefore A = 20.

**Step 2:** Measure the distance of either the upper or lower wheel (in inches). Let's say it measures 12¾", therefore B = 12¾ = 12.75.

**Step 3:** Apply the formula.
L = (2 × A) + (3.14 × B)
L = (2 × 20) + (3.14 × 12.75)
L = 40 + 40.035
L = 80.035"
You'll want to buy the nearest standard blade length—in this case, 80".

*Part Three*
**USING MATH IN THE WOODSHOP**

## Pulley Formulas

Table saws, bandsaws, jointers, drill presses and lathes often incorporate a pair of pulleys and a V-belt to transfer power from the motor to the business end of the machine. When two pulleys operate from a common V-belt, they relate to each other according to the following formula:

$A \times B = C \times D$

A = speed (in rpms) of the motor

B = diameter (in inches) of the driver (motor) pulley

C = speed (in rpms) of the driven pulley

D = diameter (in inches) of the driven pulley

Note: The motor speed (in rpms) is usually stamped on the motor nameplate.

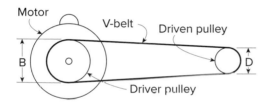

The previous formula can be rewritten, producing four additional formulas as follows:

$$A = \frac{C \times D}{B}$$

$$B = \frac{C \times D}{A}$$

$$C = \frac{A \times B}{D}$$

$$D = \frac{A \times B}{C}$$

## *Using the Pulley Formula*

The motor on a lathe operates at 1725 rpm and has a 4"-diameter pulley. The motor pulley is connected by V-belt to a 2" pulley that turns the lathe headstock. What is the lathe speed?

Based on the information, the following is known:

A = 1725 rpm

B = 4"

C = driven pulley speed = lathe speed

D = 2"

Since C is unknown, use the formula:

$$C = \frac{A \times B}{D}$$

$$= \frac{1725 \times 4}{2}$$

$$= \frac{6900}{2}$$

$$= 3450 \text{ rpm}$$

USING MATH IN THE WOODSHOP

*Part Three*

## Jointer Cutterhead-Speed Formula (In Revolutions per Minute)

See Pulley Formulas and solve for C.

## Jointer Cutterhead-Speed Formula (In Cuts per Minute)

CPM = A × N where:
A = revolutions per minute (determined from pulley formula)
N = number of jointer blades

### EXAMPLE:

You have used the pulley formula to determine your jointer cutterhead spins at 4140 rpm. The cutterhead has three blades. How many cuts per minute are produced by the cutterhead?

**Step 1:** Write the formula:
CPM = A × N

**Step 2:** Plug in the knowns:
A = 4140
N = 3
CPM = 4140 × 3
CPM = 12,420
The jointer makes 12,420 cuts per minute.

## Jointer Cutterhead-Speed Formula (In Cuts per Inch)

$$CPI = \frac{CPM}{(F \times 12)}$$ where:

CPI = jointer cuts per inch
CPM = jointer cuts per minute
F = feed rate from chart (feet per minute)

### Feed-Rate Chart

Use this chart to determine the feed rate based on the rate at which you feed the stock across the jointer cutterhead. In practice, because most woodworkers don't use a power-feeder that gets you a consistent speed, the feed rate will vary somewhat. But you can get a close approximation simply by timing the number of seconds it takes to feed a board for one foot of travel and then using the chart's right-hand column to find the equivalent feed rate in feet per minute.

| Time (In Seconds) to Feed a Board 1 Foot | Feed Rate (In Feet per Minute) |
|---|---|
| 1 | 60 |
| 2 | 30 |
| 3 | 20 |
| 4 | 15 |
| 5 | 12 |
| 6 | 10 |
| 8 | 7½ |
| 10 | 6 |

### EXAMPLE:

You are using your jointer to flatten one face of a board. Using the earlier formula, you determined that your jointer cuts at a rate of 12,420 cuts per minute (CPM). You feed the board at about 4 seconds per foot; using the chart, you determine the feed rate is 15 feet per minute. How many cuts per inch are on the board?

**Step 1:** Write the formula:

$$CPI = \frac{CPM}{(F \times 12)}$$

**Step 2:** Determine the knowns:
CPM = 12,420
F = 15

**Step 3:** Plug in the knowns and solve:

$$CPI = \frac{12,420}{(15 \times 12)}$$

$$CPI = \frac{12,420}{180}$$

CPI = 69 cuts per inch

## Bandsaw Blade Speed Formula

(For bandsaws with a pair of same-size wheels.)

$$S = \frac{(0.262 \times A \times B \times C)}{D} \quad \text{where:}$$

S = speed of bandsaw blade in feet per minute
A = diameter of bandsaw wheel (inches)
B = motor speed in revolutions per minute (rpm)
C = diameter of motor pulley (inches)
D = diameter of wheel pulley (inches)

**EXAMPLE:**
A bandsaw has 12½"-diameter wheels and a motor speed of 1725 rpm. The motor pulley is 2½" diameter; the wheel pulley is 5" diameter. What is the blade speed in feet per minute?

**Step 1:** Write the formula:

$$S = \frac{(0.262 \times A \times B \times C)}{D}$$

**Step 2:** Determine the knowns:
A = 12½ (12.5)
B = 1725
C = 2½ (2.5)
D = 5

**Step 3:** Plug in the knowns and solve:

$$S = \frac{(0.262 \times 12.5 \times 1725 \times 2.5)}{5}$$

$$S = \frac{14,123}{5}$$

S = 2,825 feet per minute

## Temperature Conversion Formulas

Use these formulas to convert from Celsius to Fahrenheit and vice versa.

To convert from Celsius to Fahrenheit use the formula:

$$F = (1.8 \times C) + 32$$

F = degrees Fahrenheit

C = degrees Celsius

*Part Three* **USING MATH IN THE WOODSHOP**

To convert from Fahrenheit to Celsius use the formula:

$$C = .556 \times (F - 32)$$

C = degrees Celsius

F = degrees Fahrenheit

---

**WOODSHOP APPLICATION**

## *Using the Temperature Conversion Formulas*

Convert 30° Celsius to Fahrenheit.

$$F = (1.8 \times C) + 32$$
$$F = (1.8 \times 30) + 32$$
$$F = 54 + 32$$
$$F = 86°$$

Convert 68° Fahrenheit to Celsius.

$$C = .556 \times (F - 32)$$
$$C = .556 \times (68 - 32)$$
$$C = .556 \times 36$$
$$C = 20°$$

---

## How to Calculate Board Feet

The board foot (bf) is a measure of volume. One board foot is equal to 144 cubic inches or a board that measures 1" thick (nominal dimension) by 12" wide (nominal dimension) by 1' long (actual dimension). The nominal dimension represents the thickness and width dimensions of a piece of lumber immediately after it is cut from a log.

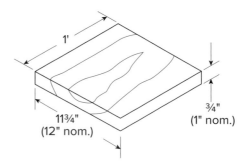

1'

11¾"
(12" nom.)

¾"
(1" nom.)

Several formulas can be used to calculate board feet, but the one most often used is as follows:

$$\text{Board feet} = \frac{\text{thickness (inches)} \times \text{width (inches)} \times \text{length (feet)}}{12}$$

To use the formula for any piece of lumber, multiply the thickness (in inches) by the width (in inches) by the length (in feet) and divide the resulting number by 12. Normal dimensions must be used for the thickness and width.

WOODSHOP APPLICATION

## *Calculating Board Feet*

How many board feet are in a 10' length of 1 × 6 lumber?

**Step 1:** Plug the numbers into the formula.

$$\text{Board feet} = \frac{1 \times 6 \times 10}{12}$$

**Step 2:** Multiply the thickness, width and length.

$$\text{Board feet} = \frac{60}{12}$$

**Step 3:** Divide the product by 12.

$$\text{Board feet} = 5$$

If you prefer to avoid math, the Board Footage Chart that follows lists board footage for a variety of board sizes and lengths.

## Board Footage Chart

| Nominal Size of Board (Inches) | Board Feet per Linear Foot | Board Feet (To Nearest 100th) Length of Board (Feet) | | | | | |
|---|---|---|---|---|---|---|---|
| | | **6** | **8** | **10** | **12** | **14** | **16** |
| ½ × 2 | 0.0833 | 0.50 | 0.67 | 0.83 | 1.00 | 1.17 | 1.33 |
| ½ × 3 | 0.1250 | 0.75 | 1.00 | 1.25 | 1.50 | 1.75 | 2.00 |
| ½ × 4 | 0.1667 | 1.00 | 1.33 | 1.67 | 2.00 | 2.33 | 2.67 |
| ½ × 6 | 0.2500 | 1.50 | 2.00 | 2.50 | 3.00 | 3.50 | 4.00 |
| ½ × 8 | 0.3333 | 2.00 | 2.67 | 3.33 | 4.00 | 4.67 | 5.33 |
| ½ × 10 | 0.4167 | 2.50 | 3.33 | 4.17 | 5.00 | 5.83 | 6.67 |
| ½ × 12 | 0.5000 | 3.00 | 4.00 | 5.00 | 6.00 | 7.00 | 8.00 |
| 1 × 2 | 0.1667 | 1.00 | 1.33 | 1.67 | 2.00 | 2.33 | 2.67 |
| 1 × 3 | 0.2500 | 1.50 | 2.00 | 2.50 | 3.00 | 3.50 | 4.00 |
| 1 × 4 | 0.3333 | 2.00 | 2.67 | 3.33 | 4.00 | 4.67 | 5.33 |
| 1 × 6 | 0.5000 | 3.00 | 4.00 | 5.00 | 6.00 | 7.00 | 8.00 |
| 1 × 8 | 0.6667 | 4.00 | 5.33 | 6.67 | 8.00 | 9.33 | 10.67 |

| Nominal Size of Board (Inches) | Board Feet per Linear Foot | Board Feet (To Nearest 100th) Length of Board (Feet) | | | | | |
|---|---|---|---|---|---|---|---|
| 1 × 10 | 0.8333 | 5.00 | 6.67 | 8.33 | 10.00 | 11.67 | 13.33 |
| 1 × 12 | 1.0000 | 6.00 | 8.00 | 10.00 | 12.00 | 14.00 | 16.00 |
| 2 × 2 | 0.3333 | 2.00 | 2.67 | 3.33 | 4.00 | 4.67 | 5.33 |
| 2 × 3 | 0.5000 | 3.00 | 4.00 | 5.00 | 6.00 | 7.00 | 8.00 |
| 2 × 4 | 0.6667 | 4.00 | 5.33 | 6.67 | 8.00 | 9.33 | 10.67 |
| 2 × 6 | 1.0000 | 6.00 | 8.00 | 10.00 | 12.00 | 14.00 | 16.00 |
| 2 × 8 | 1.3333 | 8.00 | 10.67 | 13.33 | 16.00 | 18.67 | 21.33 |
| 2 × 10 | 1.6667 | 10.00 | 13.33 | 16.67 | 20.00 | 23.33 | 26.67 |
| 2 × 12 | 2.0000 | 12.00 | 16.00 | 20.00 | 24.00 | 28.00 | 32.00 |
| 2 × 14 | 2.3333 | 14.00 | 18.67 | 23.33 | 28.00 | 32.67 | 37.33 |
| 3 × 3 | 0.7500 | 4.50 | 6.00 | 7.50 | 9.00 | 10.50 | 12.00 |
| 3 × 4 | 1.0000 | 6.00 | 8.00 | 10.00 | 12.00 | 14.00 | 16.00 |
| 3 × 6 | 1.5000 | 9.00 | 12.00 | 15.00 | 18.00 | 21.00 | 24.00 |
| 3 × 8 | 2.0000 | 12.00 | 16.00 | 20.00 | 24.00 | 28.00 | 32.00 |
| 3 × 10 | 2.5000 | 15.00 | 20.00 | 25.00 | 30.00 | 35.00 | 40.00 |
| 3 × 12 | 3.0000 | 18.00 | 24.00 | 30.00 | 36.00 | 42.00 | 48.00 |
| 3 × 14 | 3.5000 | 21.00 | 28.00 | 35.00 | 42.00 | 49.00 | 56.00 |
| 3 × 16 | 4.000 | 24.00 | 32.00 | 40.00 | 48.00 | 56.00 | 64.00 |
| 4 × 4 | 1.3333 | 8.00 | 10.67 | 13.33 | 16.00 | 18.67 | 21.33 |
| 4 × 6 | 2.0000 | 12.00 | 16.00 | 20.00 | 24.00 | 28.00 | 32.00 |
| 4 × 8 | 2.6667 | 16.00 | 21.33 | 26.67 | 32.00 | 37.33 | 42.67 |
| 4 × 10 | 3.3333 | 20.00 | 26.67 | 33.33 | 40.00 | 46.67 | 53.33 |
| 4 × 12 | 4.0000 | 24.00 | 32.00 | 40.00 | 48.00 | 56.00 | 64.00 |
| 6 × 6 | 3.0000 | 18.00 | 24.00 | 30.00 | 36.00 | 42.00 | 48.00 |
| 6 × 8 | 4.0000 | 24.00 | 32.00 | 40.00 | 48.00 | 56.00 | 64.00 |
| 6 × 10 | 5.0000 | 30.00 | 40.00 | 50.00 | 60.00 | 70.00 | 80.00 |
| 6 × 12 | 6.0000 | 36.00 | 48.00 | 60.00 | 72.00 | 84.00 | 96.00 |

## Calculating the Weight of a Board Foot

It's often useful to know the weight of a project. For example, if you know the weight of a wall cabinet, you'll be better able to select a hanging system that provides adequate support for both the cabinet and its expected contents. If you plan to ship a project, commercial shippers want to know the project's weight. It's always a good idea to know the weight of a large project, like a chest of drawers, before you start muscling it around the woodshop. Indeed, if the calculations show the chest is going to be a backbreaker, you can enlist helpers before moving the piece around.

In most books and technical tables, the weights of various wood species are shown in terms of either the *density* or the *specific gravity*. An abbreviated specific gravity table, listing some commonly used woods, is included in this manual. You'll find more extensive tables in books on the subject of wood identification. Check your library.

Density is a measure of a material's weight per unit volume, usually shown as weight per cubic foot or, in the metric system, as kilograms per cubic meter. Unlike many other materials, wood is hygroscopic, which means it takes on or gives off water based on the relative humidity of the surrounding air. Wood densities, therefore, are a measure of the weight of the wood material and the water in the wood. Since the weight of wood can change when the relative humidity changes, most tables specify the densities at a particular moisture content.

The specific gravity provides another way to look at density. As a general definition, the specific gravity of any solid or liquid is the ratio of the density of the material to the density of water. In most technical tables, when considering wood, the cubic foot is used as the measure of volume; therefore, the specific gravity is often defined as the ratio of a cubic foot of wood to a cubic foot of water. To account for the hygroscopic characteristics of wood, most technical tables indicate specific gravity based on weight when oven-dry and volume when at 12 percent moisture content.

Keep in mind that specific gravity is based on average species characteristics, which means that the number could vary a bit from board to board.

### Some Useful Formulas Related to Density, Specific Gravity and the Weight of Wood

To calculate the density when you know the specific gravity, use this formula:

$$D = S \times 62.4$$

D = the density of wood (in pounds per cubic foot)

S = the average specific gravity of oven-dry wood

**EXAMPLE:**
Eastern white pine has an average specific gravity of .35 (at oven-dry weight and volume at 12 percent moisture content). What is the density?

$$D = .35 \times 62.4$$

$$D = 21.84 \text{ pounds per cubic foot}$$

To calculate the average specific gravity when you know the density, use this formula:

$$S = \frac{D}{62.4}$$

S = the average specific of oven-dry wood
D = the density of wood (in pounds per cubic foot)

**EXAMPLE:**
The density of black cherry (at oven-dry weight and volume at 12 percent moisture content) is 31.2 pounds per cubic foot. What is the average specific gravity?

$$S = \frac{31.2}{62.4}$$

$$S = .5$$

To calculate the weight of a board foot (in pounds) when you know the density, use this formula:

$$W = \frac{D}{12}$$

W = weight of a board foot (in pounds)
D = density of the wood (in pounds per cubic foot)

**EXAMPLE:**
White oak has a density of 42.4 pounds per cubic foot (at oven-dry weight and volume at 12 percent moisture content). What is the weight of one board foot?

$$W = \frac{42.4}{12}$$

W = 3.53 pounds per board foot

To calculate the weight of a board foot (in pounds) when you know the average specific gravity, use this formula.

$$W = \frac{S \times 62.4}{12}$$

W = weight of a board foot (in pounds)
S = average specific gravity of the wood species
   when oven-dry

**EXAMPLE:**
The average specific gravity of black walnut is .55 (at oven-dry weight and volume at 12 percent moisture content). What is the weight of one board foot?

$$W = \frac{.55 \times 62.4}{12}$$

$$W = \frac{34.32}{12}$$

W = 2.86 pounds per board foot

## Table of Specific Gravity

| Common Name | Botanical Name | Average Specific Gravity* |
|---|---|---|
| Ash (White) | *Fraxinus americana* | .60 |
| Basswood | *Tilia americana* | .37 |
| Beech | *Fagus grandifolia* | .64 |
| Birch (Yellow) | *Betula alleghaniensis* | .62 |
| Butternut | *Juglans cinerea* | .38 |
| Cedar (Eastern Red) | *Juniperus virginiana* | .47 |
| Cherry (Black) | *Prunus serotina* | .50 |
| Chestnut (American) | *Castenea dentata* | .43 |
| Douglas Fir | *Pseudotsuga menziesii* | .48 |
| Ebony | *Diospyros spp.* | .90 |
| Lignum Vitae | *Guaiacum spp.* | 1.14 |
| Mahogany (African) | *Khaya spp.* | .63 |
| Maple (Red) | *Acer rubrum* | .54 |
| Maple (Sugar) | *Acer saccharum* | .63 |
| Oak (Northern Red) | *Quercus rubra* | .63 |
| Oak (White) | *Quercus alba* | .68 |
| Pine (Idaho White) | *Pinus monticola* | .38 |
| Pine (Eastern White) | *Pinus strobes* | .35 |
| Pine (Longleaf) | *Pinus palustris* | .58 |
| Pine (Ponderosa) | *Pinus ponderosa* | .40 |
| Pine (Shortleaf) | *Pinus echinata* | .51 |
| Pine (Sugar) | *Pinus lambertiana* | .36 |
| Poplar (Yellow) | *Lirodendron tulipifera* | .42 |
| Redwood | *Sequoia sempervirens* | .40 |
| Spruce (Sitka) | *Picea sitchensis* | .40 |
| Teak | *Tectona grandis* | .57 |
| Walnut (Black) | *Juglans nigra* | .55 |
| *At oven-dry weight and volume at 12 percent moisture content | | |

USING MATH IN THE WOODSHOP · *Part Three*

WOODSHOP APPLICATION

# Determining the Weight of a Tabletop

A rectangular tabletop made from 1" (nominal thickness) black cherry measures 3' wide and 6' long. What is the approximate weight of the tabletop?

**Step 1:** Determine the number of board feet in the tabletop. (Helpful hint: Consider the tabletop as one big board and apply the board footage formula to the entire tabletop.)

$$\text{board feet} = \frac{\text{thickness (inches)} \times \text{width (inches)} \times \text{length (feet)}}{12}$$

$$= \frac{1 \times 36 \times 6}{12}$$

$$= \frac{216}{12} = 18 \text{ board feet}$$

**Step 2:** Use the table to find the average specific gravity of black cherry. According to the table, black cherry has an average specific gravity of 0.50.

**Step 3:** Apply the formula to determine the weight per board foot.

$$W = \frac{.50 \times 62.4}{12}$$

$$W = \frac{31.2}{12}$$

$$W = 2.60 \text{ pounds per board foot}$$

**Step 4:** Multiply the board footage of the tabletop by the weight per board foot.

$$18 \times 2.60 = 46.8 \text{ pounds}$$

The tabletop weighs 46.8 pounds based on an oven-dry (zero moisture content) weight. Since the actual moisture content of the tabletop is likely to be in the 6 to 12 percent range, you can expect the tabletop to weigh slightly more than the calculated amount.

## Calculating Wood Movement

### How to Calculate the Amount a Board Will Expand and Contract in Width

If you look at a board under a microscope, you'll see that the wood consists of countless tiny elongated cells, all parallel to each other and butting end to end. When woodworkers talk about *grain direction* of a board, they are referring to the direction that's parallel to all those elongated cells.

The width of a board is always measured across (perpendicular to) the grain direction of the board. The length of a board is measured parallel to the grain direction.

As the relative humidity in the air increases, those wood cells absorb the moisture in the air and get fatter. When the relative humidity goes down, the cells become drier and skinnier. The length of the cells, though, stays essentially the same.

The fact that wood cells have the ability to gain or lose moisture due to changes in the relative humidity is important to woodworkers, as it explains why a board can measure, say, 12" wide in January and 12¼" wide in July.

The reason is because, in July, the air tends to be humid in most areas of the United States (the southwest U.S. is the main exception), so the cells absorb the moisture and fatten. The cumulative effect of thousands of cells getting minutely fatter makes the board grow wider.

Come January, when the in-home air is relatively dry (exceptions being the coastline of the southeast U.S. and a few other places), much of the moisture in the cells evaporates and they shrink, causing the board to contract and become narrower. The cycle repeats year after year.

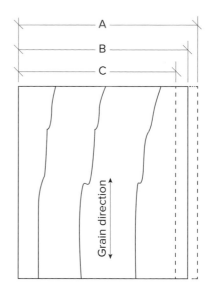

A = Width in summer (July) when wood has highest moisture content
B = Width in spring and fall
C = Width In winter (January) when wood has lowest moisture content

The thickness of a board also changes as the cells grow or shrink in size. But, because most furniture is made using relatively thin stock (2" or less, and most often 1" or less), the amount it changes in thickness is negligible. And, as already mentioned, the length stays essentially the same.

If you're working with wide boards (typically 5" and wider) it's important to pay attention to this annual cycle of changes in board width, otherwise your projects could have some unhappy surprises. Drawers get stuck in drawer openings, tabletops crack, frame members get pushed apart by panels and the list goes on.

So it helps to be able to predict how much a wide board is going to change in width during the course of a year. Armed with such information,

USING MATH IN THE WOODSHOP

*Part Three*

you can allow for those width changes when designing your joinery. Thankfully, there's no need for a crystal ball to predict wood movement; all that's required is a moisture meter and the two easy-to-use math formulas shown here. If you don't have a moisture meter, you can determine the moisture content from an oven-dried sample of the wood as described earlier.

When using the formulas, you'll need to refer to the two U.S. maps shown below and also the Movement Value Chart. The maps—one for January, one for July—provide the approximate moisture content of interior wood throughout the continental United States. The Movement Value Chart is based on two things: the wood species and the end-grain orientation (flatsawn or quartersawn). When in doubt about grain orientation, use the more conservative flatsawn value. Also, keep in mind that the formula only works when the moisture content of the wood falls within the typically common limits of 4 percent to 14 percent.

Keep in mind, too, that adding a finish to wood reduces the amount of moisture that gets into the cells. That helps reduce the amount of expansion and contraction. As a general rule, waxes and oils have the least benefit here; shellacs, varnishes, and lacquers offer somewhat more protection. Most woodworkers simply consider this extra benefit of a finish as a kind of built-in wood-movement safety factor.

Finally, it's important to remember that values from the maps and chart are based on averages, so the formula results should be considered only as good approximations.

**Formula 1:** Use this formula to determine the approximate maximum *expansion* of a board from its current width.

$$A = B \times [C \times (D - E)] \qquad \text{where:}$$

A = maximum expansion of board (in inches)
B = movement value (from chart)
C = width of board
D = highest average-moisture-content for your
    geographical region (see July map)
E = current moisture content of board as
    measured by moisture meter

### AVERAGE WOOD MOISTURE CONTENT (M.C.) THROUGHOUT THE CONTINENTAL U.S.

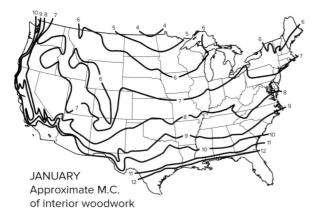

JANUARY
Approximate M.C.
of interior woodwork

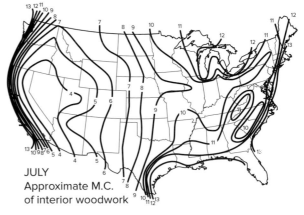

JULY
Approximate M.C.
of interior woodwork

*Part Three*
**USING MATH IN THE WOODSHOP**

**EXAMPLE:**

You live in eastern Wisconsin and want to know how much a 32"-wide, flat-sawn, red oak tabletop will expand and contract in the course of a year. A check with a moisture meter shows your board currently has a moisture content of 8 percent. To find out how much it will expand in width when July arrives:

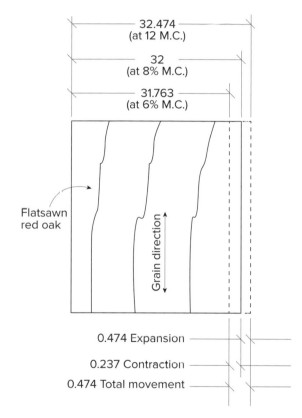

32.474 (at 12 M.C.)

32 (at 8% M.C.)

31.763 (at 6% M.C.)

Flatsawn red oak

Grain direction

0.474 Expansion

0.237 Contraction

0.474 Total movement

**Step 1:** Write Formula 1.

$A = B \times [C \times (D - E)]$

**Step 2:** Determine what you know.

B = 0.0037
C = 32
D (from July map in eastern Wisconsin) = 12
E (from moisture meter reading) = 8

**Step 3:** Plug in the knowns and solve the formula.

$A = 0.0037 \times [32 \times (12 - 8)]$
$A = 0.0037 \times [32 \times 4]$
$A = 0.0037 \times 128$
$A = 0.4736$ in. (round to 0.474)

So, come July, the board will measure approximately 32" plus 0.474" or 32.474".

**Formula 2:** Use this formula to determine the approximate maximum *contraction* (shrinkage) of a board from its current width.

$X = B \times [C \times (E - Y)]$

where:

X = maximum contraction of board (in inches)
B = movement value (from chart)
C = width of board
E = current moisture content of board as measured by moisture meter
Y = lowest average moisture content for geographical region (see January map)

USING MATH IN THE WOODSHOP

*Part Three*

**EXAMPLE**

Now you want to know how much your 32"-wide, flat-sawn, red oak board with a current moisture content of 8 percent is going to contract by the time January comes around.

**Step 1:** Write Formula 2.
$X = B \times [C \times (E - Y)]$

**Step 2:** Determine what you know.
B = 0.0037
C = 32
E (from moisture meter reading) = 8
Y (from January map in eastern Wisconsin) = 6

**Step 3:** Plug in the knowns and solve the formula.
$X = 0.0037 \times [32 \times (8 - 6)]$
$X = 0.0037 \times [32 \times 2]$
$X = 0.0037 \times 64$
X = 0.2368 in. (round to 0.237)
Come January the board will measure 32" minus 0.237", or 31.763".
To recap, in July, the 32"-wide board will measure 32.474" wide; in January it will be 31.763" wide.

**EXAMPLE**

Let's look at one more example using Formulas 1 and 2 in a slightly different way.

You live in western Massachusetts and a small chest you are building requires a drawer to fit an 8"-high drawer opening. The drawer front is to be made from flatsawn black walnut. A check with a moisture meter shows the walnut has a moisture content of 7 percent. How wide do you cut the drawer front so that in the summertime it fits in the opening as snugly as possible without sticking?

The first thing to do is find out how much an 8"-wide drawer front will expand when the humid days of July come around. That number will be the amount you want to trim from the 8"-wide drawer front so it has room for that expected expansion. To calculate expansion, you'll need to use Formula 1.

**Step 1:** Write Formula 1.
$A = B \times [C \times (D - E)]$

**Step 2:** Determine the knowns.
B (from chart) = 0.0027
C = 8
D (from July map in western Massachusetts) = 12
E = 7

**Step 3:** Plug in the knowns and solve the formula.
$A = 0.0027 \times [8 \times (12 - 7)]$
$A = 0.0027 \times [8 \times 5]$
$A = 0.0027 \times 40$
A = 0.108"

So you'll want to trim 0.108" (round it to ⅛" to provide a little extra space) from the 8" wide drawer front. That way, come July, when it's fully expanded, it won't push against the drawer opening and get stuck.

Now, working with the new drawer width of 7⅞", use Formula 2 to determine how much gap there will be when it's fully contracted in January.

**Step 1:** Write Formula 2.
$X = B \times [C \times (E - Y)]$

**Step 2:** Determine the knowns.
B (from chart) = 0.0027
C = 7⅞ (7.875 in decimal form)
E = 7
Y (from January map in western Massachusetts) = 6

**Step 3:** Plug in the knowns and solve the formula.
X = 0.0027 × [7.875 × (7 − 6)]
X = 0.0027 × [7.875 × 1]
X = 0.0027 × 7.875
X = 0.021 inches

Subtracting 0.021" from the 7⅞" (7.875") wide drawer, you get 7.854".

To summarize, you cut the drawer front with a moisture content of 7 percent to 7⅞" wide (7.875") to fit in the 8"-wide drawer opening. When July arrives, the drawer front will have expanded by 0.108" to end up at 7.983" (the sum of 7.875" and 0.108"). That leaves an acceptable gap between the top edge of the drawer front and the underside of the 8" drawer opening of slightly over 1⁄64".

Then, come January, the drawer front will have shrunk to 7.854". That's a reasonable gap in the 8" drawer opening of 0.146" or slightly less than 5⁄32". To put it another way, in the summertime there's a gap of 1⁄64"; in the wintertime the gap is 5⁄32".

## Movement Value (B)

| Wood Species | Flatsawn | Quartersawn |
| --- | --- | --- |
| Ader (Red) | 0.0026 | 0.0015 |
| Ash (Black) | 0.0027 | 0.0017 |
| Ash (White) | 0.0027 | 0.0017 |
| Aspen (Quaking) | 0.0023 | 0.0012 |
| Basswood (American) | 0.0033 | 0.0023 |
| Beech (American) | 0.0043 | 0.0019 |
| Birch (Yellow) | 0.0034 | 0.0026 |
| Butternut | 0.0022 | 0.0012 |
| Cedar (Western Red) | 0.0023 | 0.0011 |
| Cherry (Black) | 0.0025 | 0.0013 |
| Chestnut | 0.0023 | 0.0012 |
| Fir (Balsam) | 0.0024 | 0.0010 |
| Locust (Black) | 0.0025 | 0.0016 |

USING MATH IN THE WOODSHOP *Part Three*

| Wood Species | Flatsawn | Quartersawn |
| --- | --- | --- |
| Mahogany | 0.0024 | 0.0017 |
| Maple (Red) | 0.0029 | 0.0014 |
| Maple (Sugar) | 0.0035 | 0.0017 |
| Oak (Red) | 0.0037 | 0.0016 |
| Oak (White) | 0.0037 | 0.0018 |
| Pine (Eastern White) | 0.0021 | 0.0007 |
| Pine (Longleaf) | 0.0026 | 0.0018 |
| Pine (Ponderosa) | 0.0022 | 0.0013 |
| Pine (Red) | 0.0025 | 0.0013 |
| Pine (Shortleaf) | 0.0027 | 0.0016 |
| Pine (Sugar) | 0.0019 | 0.0010 |
| Poplar (Yellow) | 0.0029 | 0.0016 |
| Redwood | 0.0023 | 0.0010 |
| Spruce (Sitka) | 0.0026 | 0.0015 |
| Sweetgum | 0.0037 | 0.0018 |
| Sycamore (American) | 0.0030 | 0.0017 |
| Teak | 0.0019 | 0.0010 |
| Walnut (Black) | 0.0027 | 0.0019 |

CHAPTER 15

# Converting a Photograph into a Dimensioned Drawing

From time to time, most woodworkers will come across a book or magazine showing a photograph of a furniture piece that would be wonderful to build—if only there were some dimensions from which to work. You might be surprised to learn that with a little savvy and the help of some simple math, almost any photograph can be coaxed into giving up some of those dimensions. The math is based on the principles of *ratio* and *proportion*.

## Ratio

A ratio compares two numbers by using division. Let's say you have a box containing 10 wood screws and 25 washers. The ratio of wood screws to washers is ¹⁰⁄₂₅. By dividing both the numerator and denominator by 5, the ratio can be reduced to ²⁄₅. Put another way, for every 2 wood screws there are 5 washers. The ratio can also be written as 2 ÷ 5 or 2:5. The symbol : is called the *ratio sign*.

In the same box, the ratio of washers to wood screws is ²⁵⁄₁₀ which reduces to ⁵⁄₂. In other words, for every 5 washers there are 2 wood screws.

Let's consider another example. The top of a coffee table measures 18" wide by 48" long. The ratio of the width to the length is ¹⁸⁄₄₈, which reduces to ³⁄₈. For every 3" of width, the tabletop has 8" of length.

For the same tabletop, the ratio of the length to the width is ⁴⁸⁄₁₈, or ⁸⁄₃. For every 8" of length, there are 3" of width.

## Proportion

A proportion shows that two ratios are equal; for example, ½ = ⁵⁄₁₀, which can also be written as 1:2 :: 5:10. The symbol :: is called the *proportion sign*. When a proportion is set up in this manner, the inside numbers (2 and 5) are called the *means*, while the outside numbers (1 and 10) are called the *extremes*. Examples of other proportions are ⅔ = ⁶⁄₉, ⅘ = ¹⁶⁄₁₀ and ¼ = ⁴⁄₁₆.

## The Cross Product Rule

The *cross product rule* states that, in any proportion, the product of the means equals the product of the extremes. Therefore:

a:b :: c:d

a/b = c/d

ad = bc

USING MATH IN THE WOODSHOP

*Part Three*

The equation can also be written as:

$$a = bc/d$$

$$b = ad/c$$

$$c = ad/b$$

$$d = bc/a$$

Let's look at the proportion 1:2 :: 5:10 and see if it checks out.

$$1:2 :: 5:10$$

$$\frac{1}{2} = \frac{5}{10}$$

$$1 \times 10 = 2 \times 5$$

$$10 = 10$$

Since 10 = 10, the ratios 1:2 and 5:10 are in proportion.

## Using Proportion to Dimension a Photograph

Let's say you spot a drop leaf table in a magazine. It's a piece you'd love to build if you had some dimensions. Here's how to get them using the principles of ratio and proportion.

**Step 1:** Find something in the photo that can provide a clue to the scale.

This step takes some creative guesswork. Begin by looking for any item in the photo that has a generally standard size. It could be a coffee mug,

a dinner plate or a hardcover book. The sizes of these items are somewhat standard:  a 4" height for a coffee mug, a 10" diameter for a dinner plate and a 10" to 12" height for a hardcover book. The item could be a nearby piece of furniture that is built to standard dimensions. For example, the seat height for a chair is usually 17" to 18½". Once you find a standard-sized item, assign it a dimension.

If you can't find a standard-sized item in the photo, you'll need to assign a dimension to some part of the piece. For example, if the piece is a wall cabinet, decide how tall or wide you want it to be, then assign a dimension to either the height or width.

All subsequent dimensions will be based on your assigned dimension, so try to be as accurate as you can. If possible, work with vertical measurements, as diagonal and horizontal measurements sometimes appear shorter due to the camera angle.

Let's say our example provides only one clue to the table's size. All tables typically measure 29" to 31" in height. Since 30" is a good average, let's go with that.

**Step 2:** Calculate the working ratio. Measure the table height directly from the photograph. Let's say it measures just about 2". Since we know the actual table height is 30", the ratio of the photo height to actual height is $\frac{2}{30}$, which reduces to $\frac{1}{15}$. This ratio, called the *working ratio,* is the one you will use to calculate all the remaining dimensions.

**Step 3:** Calculate the tabletop length. Next, measure the table length directly from the photograph. Let's say it measures about 4". The cross product rule can now be applied, since you know three of the four items.

$$\frac{a}{b} = \frac{c}{d}$$

a = 1"

b = 15"

c = 4"

d = unknown

$$\frac{1}{15} = \frac{4}{d}$$

Using the cross product formula for d:

$$d = \frac{bc}{a}$$

$$d = \frac{15 \times 4}{1}$$

d = 60"

The tabletop is 60" long.

**Step 4:** Calculate the width of the drop leaves. Measure the width of the front drop leaf directly from the photograph. Let's say it measures ⅝". Applying the cross product rule you have:

$$\frac{a}{b} = \frac{c}{d}$$

a = 1"

b = 15"

c = ⅝" = .625"

d = unknown

Using the cross product formula for d:

$$d = \frac{bc}{a}$$

$$d = \frac{15 \times .625}{1}$$

d = 9.375" = 9⅜"

Each drop leaf is 9⅜" wide.

**Step 5:** Determine the width of the tabletop. Because of the camera angle, the tabletop width appears shortened in our example photo. Since there is no way to measure the full width of the tabletop from the photo, you'll need to come up with a dimension on your own.

USING MATH IN THE WOODSHOP

*Part Three*

As a general rule, a drop leaf table like this will have a tabletop width that measures about twice the width of a leaf. Or, to put it another way, the ratio of tabletop width to leaf width is 2:1. Since you know the actual width of the leaf, you can use the cross product formula to find the width of the tabletop.

Applying the cross product rule you have:

$$\frac{a}{b} = \frac{c}{d}$$

a = 2

b = 1

c = unknown

d = 9⅜ = 9.375"

Using the cross product formula for c:

$$c = \frac{ad}{b}$$

$$c = \frac{2 \times 9.375}{1}$$

c = 18.75" = 18¾" wide

The tabletop measures 18¾" wide

**Step 6:** Calculate the upper width of the tapered leg.

In our imaginary example, the drop leaf covers the upper part of the tapered leg, so measure the leg width at the highest visible point. Let's say it measures about ⅞₄" wide.

Applying the cross product formula rule you have:

$$\frac{a}{b} = \frac{c}{d}$$

a = 1"

b = 15"

c = ⁷⁄₆₄" = .109375"

d = unknown

Using the cross product formula for d:

$$d = \frac{bc}{a}$$

$$d = \frac{15 \times .109375}{1}$$

d = 1.641", or just under 1¹¹⁄₁₆".

Since the tapered leg is going to be slightly wider above the point where it was measured on the photograph, it's a pretty safe assumption that the leg is made from 1¾"-wide stock. Also, since legs on similar tables are almost always made from square stock, it can be reasonably assumed that the legs are made from 1¾"-square stock.

**Step 7:** Calculate the lower width of the tapered leg.

Assume the lower end of the leg measures about ⅟₁₆".

Applying the cross product rule you have:

$$\frac{a}{b} = \frac{c}{d}$$

a = 1"

b = 15"

c = ⅟₁₆" = .0625"

d = unknown

Using the cross product formula for d:

$$d = \frac{bc}{a}$$

$$d = \frac{15 \times .0625}{1}$$

d = .9375" (round to 1")

The leg tapers to 1" at the bottom. (Typically, tables like this have legs that are tapered on only two inside faces, rather than on all four faces.)

**Step 8:** Determine the width of the aprons.
The leaves prevent you from seeing the table frame, but drop leaf tables usually use four aprons to tie the legs together. For a table this size, 5"-wide aprons should provide adequate strength.

**Step 9:** Determine the apron joinery.
Dowels can be used to join the end of each apron to a leg, but a mortise-and-tenon joint is more traditional and will provide greater strength.

**Step 10:** Determine the drop leaf support system.
The drop leaf support system is completely hidden by the front leaf in the photograph. To find out how to build such a system, you'll need to consult a good woodworking design book. Several simple systems are commonly used.

## Ratio and the Golden Rectangle

Rectangular shapes are everywhere. We see them in art, architecture, engineering and, of course, woodworking. The rectangle is the basic shape for all sorts of furniture—desks, tables and cabinets to name a few. Many components of a furniture piece—doors, drawers, tops, sides and the like—are often rectangles, too.

Rectangles come in an endless number of shapes; from long and thin to short and fat. But of all the possible shapes, there is one in particular that our eyes find especially pleasing. It's called the *golden rectangle,* although it's also known as the golden section, golden mean, golden number, divine proportion, divine section and golden proportion. In any golden rectangle, the ratio of the short side to the long side is 1 : 1.618.

**USING MATH IN THE WOODSHOP**

*Part Three*

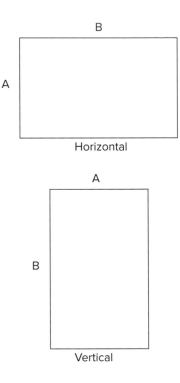

B

A

**Horizontal**

A

B

**Vertical**

The Parthenon in Greece is often cited as having proportions based on the golden rectangle. So too are playing cards, credit cards, and 3 x 5 postcards (actually 1 : 1.667). The flag of the United States has a width-to-length ratio of 1 : 9, close to the Golden Rectangle. The proportions of the United Nations building in New York City is also claimed to closely match the golden rectangle.

To create a golden rectangle of any size, use this formula when you know the length of the long side and want to determine the length of the short side:
A = B / 1.618
where:
A = short side
B = long side

Use this formula when you know the length of the short side and want to determine the length of the long side:
B = A × 1.618

**EXAMPLE 1**
You're designing an end table and want a 12"-long drawer front to have the shape of a golden rectangle. How high must it be?

**Step 1:** Use the formula: A = B / 1.618

**Step 2:** Plug in the known: A = 12 / 1.618
A = 7.417 (round to 7½")

**EXAMPLE 2**
A cabinet door is 17" wide. How tall must it be to create a golden rectangle?

**Step 1:** Use the formula: B = A × 1.618

**Step 2:** Plug in the known: B = 17 × 1.618
B = 27.506 (round to 27½")

*Part Three* **USING MATH IN THE WOODSHOP**

CHAPTER 16

# Reading Micrometers and Dial Calipers

Carpenter's rules, tape measures and steel rules are the workhorses when it comes to measuring in the woodshop. Although most of these tools are, at best, accurate to ⅟₆₄", that's sufficient accuracy for most woodshop applications. Occasionally, however, it can be valuable to measure more accurately and that's where a micrometer or caliper can come in handy. Indeed, most micrometers and calipers are accurate to ⅟₁₀₀₀" (.001").

Micrometers and calipers can be put to good use measuring the thickness of veneer, sheet metal, plastic laminate (e.g., Formica), acrylic sheet (e.g. Plexiglas), thin plywood and miscellaneous hardware, including hinges. In addition, the measuring tools can be used to accurately check the diameters of bolts, screws, nails, brads, machine threads and the like. Calipers, which can also check inside diameters, are ideally suited for measuring drilled holes, the inside diameters of bushings and the widths of dadoes and grooves.

## The Micrometer

The micrometer is a precision instrument for measuring thicknesses and diameters (Fig. 16-1). Indeed, you'll find most models are accurate to ⅟₁₀₀₀" (.001"), which is plenty accurate for woodshop applications. Metric models are also available, but our discussion will be limited to micrometers that measure in inches. Micrometers are sold in a variety of size ranges: 0" to ½", 0" to 1", 1" to 2", 2" to 3", and so on, up to 23" to 24". In the woodshop, the micrometer is used mostly for taking small measurements, so the 0" to 1" size range generally proves to be the most practical size.

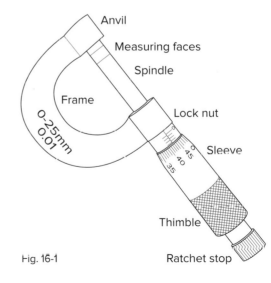

Fig. 16-1

**USING MATH IN THE WOODSHOP**    *Part Three*

## Reading the Micrometer

With an array of moving parts and numbered lines, the micrometer might look a little imposing to the uninitiated. Actually, I think you'll find it's easy to read. Basically you work with just two numbered lines: those on the sleeve and those on the thimble (Fig. 16-2).

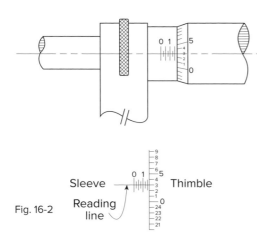

Fig. 16-2

Sleeve    Thimble

Reading line

## Lines on the Sleeves

The reading line on the sleeve, as shown in Fig. 16-2, is divided into 40 parts, each part representing 0.25. Micrometers are designed so one full revolution of the thimble moves the spindle face .025". Every fourth line is extended and represents 4 × .025 or $\frac{100}{1000}$ (.100").

The extended lines on the sleeve are marked 0, 1, 2, 3, 4 and so on through 10. The line marked 1 represents $\frac{100}{1000}$" (.100"), the line marked 2 represents $\frac{200}{1000}$" (.200"), the line marked 3 represents $\frac{300}{1000}$" (.300") and so on, through 10, which represents $\frac{1000}{1000}$" or 1".

## Lines on the Thimble

As shown in Fig. 16-2, the circumference of the thimble is divided into 25 equal parts, numbered from 0 to 25, with each part representing $\frac{1}{1000}$" (.001"). The line marked 1 represents $\frac{1}{1000}$" (.001"), the line marked 2 represents $\frac{2}{1000}$" (.002") and so on, through 25, which completes a revolution of the thimble and represents $\frac{25}{1000}$" (.025").

## Taking a Measurement

When measuring most small parts, the micrometer is held as shown in Fig. 16-3. Place the part against the micrometer anvil with the left hand, then use the thumb and index finger of your right hand to turn the thimble. Turn the thimble until the face of the spindle lightly contacts the part. Take the reading while the part remains in the micrometer. lock the spindle at the final setting, then remove the part and take the reading.

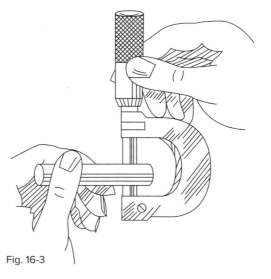

Fig. 16-3

Here's how to read a micrometer:

*Part Three*
**USING MATH IN THE WOODSHOP**

**Step 1:** Read the sleeve. To do this, multiply the number of vertical divisions on the sleeve by .025".

**Step 2:** Read the thimble by determining the thimble number that aligns with the reading on the sleeve. Multiply the number by .001.

**Step 3:** Add the product from step one to the product from step two. Let's look at an example.

**EXAMPLE:** *Read the micrometer setting shown in Fig. 16-2.*

**Step 1:** Read the sleeve. Seven vertical divisions are visible, so 7 × .025 = .175".

**Step 2:** Read the thimble. The number three aligns with the reading line on the sleeve. Each number represents .001, therefore 3 × .001 = .003".

**Step 3:** Add the product from step one to the product in step two.

$$\begin{array}{r} .175 \\ + .003 \\ \hline .178 \end{array}$$

The micrometer reads .178".

## The Dial Caliper

In recent years, the dial caliper (Fig. 16-4) has become considerably more popular than the vernier caliper. The reason is simple: compared to the vernier caliper, a dial caliper is much easier to use. A 6" dial caliper is the size most commonly found in woodworking shops.

Since many woodworkers find it easier to work in fractions rather than decimals, some manufacturers are now offering dial calipers that read both decimals and fractions. Fig. 16-4 shows one. The decimal scale reads in increments of 0.010", while the fractional scale reads in increments of ⅟₆₄". If you prefer to work in increments 0.001", you'll probably need a decimal-only caliper.

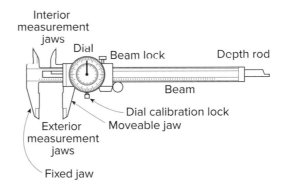

Fig. 16-4

### Reading the Dial Caliper

Numbers show up in only two places on a dial caliper—in the beam and on the dial. To determine a measurement you simply read the numbers on each part and add them together.

USING MATH IN THE WOODSHOP

*Part Three*

## Lines on the Beam

On the dial caliper shown in Fig. 16-4, the bottom edge of the beam has a series of marked lines that extend for 6". The 6" length is divided into six 1"-long parts. Each 1"-long part is divided into ten evenly spaced parts marked by a single line. So, each line on the beam equals ¹⁄₁₀", or 0.100".

## Lines on the Dial

The dial on a decimal/fraction caliper has two scales: an outside decimal scale, and an inside fractional scale. The outside is divided into 100 evenly spaced parts, with each part equal to ¹⁄₁₀₀" or 0.01". The inside scale is divided into 64 evenly spaced parts, with each part equal to ¹⁄₆₄". On the inside scale, starting from zero, every eighth increment is shown as a fraction: ⅛, ¼, ⅜, ½, ⅝, ¾ and ⅞.

As you slide the movable jaw away from the fixed measuring jaw, the hand rotates clockwise, with each full revolution of the hand adding 1" to the length. Slide the jaw closer to the fixed jaw and the hands move in a counter-clockwise direction.

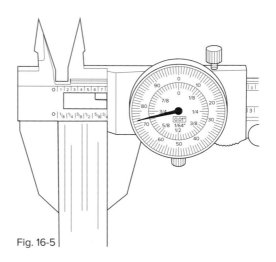

Fig. 16-5

## Taking a Measurement

As was the case when using the vernier caliper, the jaws of a dial caliper should only lightly touch the part to be measured.

Here's how to read a typical decimal/fraction dial caliper.

**EXAMPLE:** *Read the dial caliper setting shown in Fig. 16-5.*

## To Read Decimals

**Step 1:** On the beam, read the number of full inches showing between the fixed and movable jaws. If less than one, use zero.

Note that it reads less than one, so use zero.

*Part Three*

**USING MATH IN THE WOODSHOP**

**Step 2:** On the outside scale of the dial, read the number pointed to by the hand. Multiply the number by 0.01".

    The hand points to the number 72 on the dial; $72 \times .01" = .72"$

**Step 3:** Add the numbers from steps 1 and 2.

$$
\begin{array}{r}
0.00 \\
+ .72 \\
\hline
0.72
\end{array}
$$

The part measures 0.72".

## To Read Fractions

**Step 1:** On the beam, read the number of full inches showing between the fixed and movable jaws.

    Note that it reads less than one, so use zero.

**Step 2:** On the inside scale of the dial, note the location of the hand. Then, reading counter-clockwise, find the nearest fraction on the scale. Convert that fraction to 64ths.

    Reading counter-clockwise from the pointer in Fig. 16-5, the nearest fraction is $\frac{5}{8}$. Convert $\frac{5}{8}$ to a fraction with a denominator of 64.

$$
\begin{aligned}
5 \times 8 &= 40 \\
8 \times 8 &= 64
\end{aligned}
$$

$$
\frac{5}{8} = \frac{40}{64}
$$

**Step 3:** On the inside scale of the dial, count the number of increments from the nearest fraction ($\frac{5}{8}$ or $\frac{40}{64}$) to the hand. Multiply the number of increments by $\frac{1}{64}$.

    There are six increments: $6 \times \frac{1}{64} = \frac{6}{64}$.

**Step 4:** Add the numbers from steps one, two and three.

$$
\frac{0}{64} + \frac{40}{64} + \frac{6}{64} = \frac{46}{64}
$$

    The measurement in fractions is $\frac{46}{64}$"; or, when reduced, $\frac{23}{32}$".

*Part Three*

**USING MATH IN THE WOODSHOP**

# APPENDIX

# *Appendix*

**Acute angle**   An angle less than 90°.

**Angle**   The space between two straight lines that meet.

**Angle sides**   The straight lines that meet to form an angle.

**Arc**   A portion of the circumference.

**Area**   A measure of the amount of surface on a figure. See *Surface area.*

**Avoirdupois**   A system of weights based on the pound system used by many English-speaking countries including the U.S.

**Base**   1. A factor that is repeatedly multiplied. 2. The end of a prism.

**Bisect**   To divide in half.

**Canceling**   A means of reducing a fraction by dividing the numerator and denominator by a common factor.

**Chord**   A straight line connecting two points on a circle.

**Circle**   A closed curve, with all points equally distant from the center.

**Circumference**   The distance around a circle.

**Common denominator**   A denominator that two or more fractions share.

**Common multiplier or common number**   A number that, when multiplied by the numerator and denominator of a fraction, raises the fraction to a higher term.

**Compound angle cut**   The angle created when a work piece is cut at an angle other than 90° using a saw blade that is also at an angle other than 90°.

**Concentric circles**   Two or more circles with the same center point but different diameters.

**Cone**   A solid with a circular base whose lateral surface narrows to a point at the top.

**Cube**   A regular solid with six square face surfaces. See *Hexahedron.*

**Cube root**   A factor multiplied three times to produce a power.

**Cylinder**   A solid bounded by two equal, parallel circles and by a curved surface formed by moving a straight line of fixed length so the ends lie on the two parallel circles.

**Decimal**   A means of expressing a fraction that has a denominator of ten or some multiple of ten.

**Decimal point**   A dot used to separate a whole number from a decimal.

**Denominator**   The bottom part of a fraction.

**Density**   A measure of a material's weight per unit volume.

**Diameter**   A straight line that passes through the center of a circle and extends from one side of the circle to the other.

**Digit**   One of the ten symbols 0 through 9.

**Dividend**   The number to be divided by another number.

**Divisor**   The number divided into another number.

**Eccentric circles**   Two or more intersecting circles with different center points.

**Ellipse**   An oval-shaped closed curve.

**Equation**   A statement showing that two numbers or two groups of numbers are equal.

**Equilateral triangle**   A triangle with sides of equal length.

**Equivalent fraction**   A fraction with the same value as another fraction.

**Expanded form**   A number broken down into its component groups of ten or multiples of ten.

**Exponent**   A small, raised (superscript) number written adjacent to a base number indicating the number of times the base number must be repeatedly multiplied.

**Factor**   A number that, when multiplied by another number, results in a product.

**Formula**   An equation that shows a unique relationship between certain things.

**Fraction**   One or more of the equal parts of a whole.

**Fraction bar or fraction line**   The short, straight line drawn between the numerator and denominator of a fraction.

**Grid square method**   A method for enlarging patterns using a grid of squares.

**Hexahedron**   A regular solid with six square face surfaces. See *Cube*.

**Horizontal line**   A straight line parallel to the horizon.

**Hypotenuse**   In a right triangle, the side opposite the right angle.

**Improper fraction**   A fraction with a numerator that is equal to or greater than the denominator.

**Index**   A small, raised number written to the left of the radical sign indicating how many times the equal factors are multiplied to produce the number within the radical sign.

**Irregular curved line**   A curved line with a radius that constantly changes.

**Isoceles triangle**   A triangle with two sides of equal length.

**Lateral face**   The side of a prism.

**LCD**   The smallest number that is evenly divisible by the denominators of a group of fractions. See *Lowest common denominator*.

**Like fractions**   Fractions with the same denominator.

**Line**   A straight line.

**Lowest common denominator**   The smallest number that is evenly divisible by the denominators of a group of fractions. See *LCD*.

**Mixed number**   A number made up of a whole number and a fraction.

**Numerator**   The top part of a fraction.

**Oblique cone**   A cone whose axis is not perpendicular to the base.

**Oblique cylinder**   A cylinder whose lateral surface is not perpendicular to the base.

**Oblique line**   A straight line that is neither horizontal nor vertical.

**Oblique rectangular prism**   A prism with lateral faces not perpendicular to a square base.

**Oblique square pyramid**   A pyramid with the axis not perpendicular to a square base.

**Obtuse angle**   An angle that is more than 90° but less than 180°.

**Obtuse triangle**   A triangle with an obtuse angle.

**Parallel lines**   Two or more straight lines that remain the same distance apart at all points.

**Perimeter**   The distance around any closed plane figure.

**Perpendicular lines**   Straight lines that intersect at 90°.

**Photocopy method**   A method for enlarging patterns using a photocopier.

**Place value**   The location of a digit in a number.

**Plane figure**   A shape that has length and width, but no depth.

**Plus sign**   The symbol (+) used to indicate a positive number or the operation of addition.

**Polygon**   A closed plane figure that has three or more sides and three or more angles.

**Power**   The product of a factor that is repeatedly multiplied.

**Prism**   A solid with two parallel bases that are identical polygons.

**Proper fraction**   A fraction with a numerator that is less than the denominator.

**Proportion**   A statement that shows two ratios are equal.

**Proportion sign**   The symbol (::) used to indicate proportion.

**Pyramid**   A solid with a polygon for its base and triangles for its sides.

**Quadrilateral**   A polygon with four sides and four angles.

**Quotient**   The number that results from the division of two numbers.

**Radical sign**   The symbol $\sqrt{\ }$ is used to indicate the root of a number.

**Radius**   A straight line extending from the center of a circle to any point on the circle.

**Ratio**   A comparison of two numbers using division.

**Rectangle**   A four-sided figure with four right angles.

**Reduced fraction**   A fraction written in its lowest number. See *Simplest form.*

**Regular decagon**   A figure having ten equal-length sides and ten equal angles.

**Regular dodecagon**   A figure having twelve equal-length sides and twelve equal angles.

**Regular hexagon**   A figure having six equal-length sides and six equal angles.

**Regular octagon**   A figure having eight equal-length sides and eight equal angles.

**Regular pentagon**   A figure having five equal-length sides and five equal angles.

**Regular polygon**   A polygon with all angles equal and all sides of equal length.

**Regular solid**   A solid with face surfaces that are regular polygons.

**Rhomboid**   A four-sided figure with opposite sides parallel, adjacent sides unequal and usually having two acute angles and two obtuse angles.

**Rhombus**   A four-sided figure with all sides of equal length, opposite sides parallel, and usually having two acute angles and two obtuse angles.

**Right angle**   The angle formed by the intersection of a straight line perpendicular to another straight line and measuring 90°.

**Right cone**   A cone with the axis perpendicular to the base.

**Right cylinder**   A cylinder whose lateral surface is perpendicular to the base.

**Right rectangular prism**   A prism with a lateral face perpendicular to a rectangular base.

**Right square prism**   A prism with a lateral face perpendicular to a square base.

**Right square pyramid**   A pyramid with the axis perpendicular to a square base.

**Right triangle**   A triangle with one 90° angle.

**Right triangle pyramid**   A pyramid with the axis perpendicular to a triangular base.

**Root (of a number)**   A factor that when repeatedly multiplied produces the number.

**Scalene triangle**   A triangle with all sides unequal in length.

**Segment**   The part of a circle cut off by a straight line.

**Semicircle**   One-half of a circle.

**Simplest form**   A fraction written in its lowest terms. See *Reduced fraction.*

**Simplifying**   The process of reducing a fraction to its lowest terms.

**Solid figure**   A shape that has length, width and depth.

**Specific gravity (of a solid or liquid)**   A ratio of the density of a material to the density of water.

**Sphere**   A round, solid figure in which every point on the surface is the same distance from the center.

**Square**   A four-sided figure with four right angles and four equal-length sides.

**Square root**   A factor of a number that when multiplied by itself gives the number.

**Straight angle**   An angle formed by two lines that intersect to form a straight line and measuring 180°.

**Straight line**   The shortest distance between two points.

**Surface area**   A measure of the amount of surface on a figure. See *Area.*

**Tangent**   A straight line that touches a circle at only one point.

**Terms**   The numerator and denominator of a fraction.

**Tetrahedron**   A regular solid with four triangular face surfaces.

**Theorem**   In geometry, any statement or rule that can be proved to be true.

**Trapezium**   A four-sided figure having no sides parallel.

**Trapezoid**   A four-sided figure with two sides parallel and two sides not parallel.

**Triangle**   A polygon with three sides and three angles.

**Triangular prism**   A prism with triangular bases.

**Trisect**   To divide into thirds.

**Truncated pyramid**   The portion that remains after a cutting plane is passed through a pyramid.

**Truncated right cone**   The portion that remains after a cutting plane is passed through a right cone.

**Unlike fractions**   Fractions with different denominators.

**Vertex**   The point where two angle sides meet to form an angle.

**Vertical line**   A straight line perpendicular to the horizon.

**Volume**   A measure of the three-dimensional size of a solid figure.

**Whole number**   Any number that is not a fraction or a decimal.

## Roman and Arabic Numerals

| Roman Numeral | Arabic Numeral | Roman Numeral | Arabic Numeral |
|---|---|---|---|
| I | 1 | XXIV | 24 |
| II | 2 | XXV | 25 |
| III | 3 | XXVI | 26 |
| IV | 4 | XXVII | 27 |
| V | 5 | XXVIII | 28 |
| VI | 6 | XXIX | 29 |
| VII | 7 | XXX | 30 |
| VIII | 8 | XL | 40 |
| IX | 9 | L | 50 |
| X | 10 | LX | 60 |
| XI | 11 | LXX | 70 |
| XII | 12 | LXXX | 80 |
| XIII | 13 | XC | 90 |
| XIV | 14 | C | 100 |
| XV | 15 | CC | 200 |
| XVI | 16 | CCC | 300 |
| XVII | 17 | CD | 400 |
| XVIII | 18 | D | 500 |
| XIX | 19 | DC | 600 |
| XX | 20 | DCC | 700 |
| XXI | 21 | DCCC | 800 |
| XXII | 22 | CM | 900 |
| XXIII | 23 | M | 1000 |

# Millimeters to Inches (Decimal Equivalents)

| Millimeters | Inches (Decimal Equivalent) |
|---|---|
| 1 | .03937 |
| 2 | .07874 |
| 3 | .11811 |
| 4 | .15748 |
| 5 | .19685 |
| 6 | .23622 |
| 7 | .27559 |
| 8 | .31496 |
| 9 | .35433 |
| 10 | .39370 |
| 11 | .43307 |
| 12 | .47244 |
| 13 | .51181 |
| 14 | .55118 |
| 15 | .59055 |
| 16 | .62992 |
| 17 | .66929 |
| 18 | .70866 |
| 19 | .74803 |
| 20 | .78740 |
| 21 | .82677 |
| 22 | .86614 |
| 23 | .90551 |
| 24 | .94488 |
| 25 | .98425 |
| 26 | 1.02362 |

## Fractions to Decimal Equivalents (Inches)

| Millimeters | Inches (Decimal Equivalent) | Millimeters | Inches (Decimal Equivalent) |
|---|---|---|---|
| 1/64 | .015625 | 27/64 | .421875 |
| 1/32 | .031250 | 7/16 | .437500 |
| 3/64 | .046875 | 29/64 | .453125 |
| 1/16 | .062500 | 15/32 | .468750 |
| 5/64 | .078125 | 31/64 | .484375 |
| 3/32 | .093750 | 1/2 | .500000 |
| 7/64 | .109375 | 33/64 | .515625 |
| 1/8 | .125000 | 17/32 | .531250 |
| 9/64 | .140625 | 35/64 | .546875 |
| 5/32 | .156250 | 9/16 | .562500 |
| 11/64 | .171875 | 37/64 | .578125 |
| 3/16 | .187500 | 19/32 | .593750 |
| 13/64 | .203125 | 39/64 | .609375 |
| 7/32 | .218750 | 5/8 | .625000 |
| 15/64 | .234375 | 41/64 | .640625 |
| 1/4 | .250000 | 21/32 | .656250 |
| 17/64 | .265625 | 43/64 | .671875 |
| 9/32 | .281250 | 11/16 | .687500 |
| 19/64 | .296875 | 45/64 | .703125 |
| 5/16 | .312500 | 23/32 | .718750 |
| 21/64 | .328125 | 47/64 | .734375 |
| 11/32 | .343750 | 3/4 | .750000 |
| 23/64 | .359375 | 49/64 | .765625 |
| 3/8 | .375000 | 25/32 | .781250 |
| 25/64 | .390625 | 51/64 | .796875 |
| 13/32 | .406250 | 13/16 | .812500 |

| Millimeters | Inches (Decimal Equivalent) |
|---|---|
| 53/64 | .828125 |
| 27/32 | .843750 |
| 55/64 | .859375 |
| 7/8 | .875000 |
| 57/64 | .890625 |
| 29/32 | .906250 |
| 59/64 | .921875 |
| 15/16 | .937500 |
| 61/64 | .953125 |
| 31/32 | .968750 |
| 63/64 | .984375 |
| 1 | 1.00000 |

## Inches to Millimeters (Fractions to Decimal Equivalents)

| Inches (Fraction) | Millimeters (Decimal Equivalent) | Inches (Fraction) | Millimeters (Decimal Equivalent) |
| --- | --- | --- | --- |
| 1/64 | 0.396875 | 27/64 | 10.71563 |
| 1/32 | 0.793750 | 7/16 | 11.11250 |
| 3/64 | 1.190625 | 29/64 | 11.50938 |
| 1/16 | 1.587500 | 15/32 | 11.90625 |
| 5/64 | 1.984375 | 31/64 | 12.30313 |
| 3/32 | 2.381250 | 1/2 | 12.70000 |
| 7/64 | 2.778125 | 33/64 | 13.09688 |
| 1/8 | 3.175000 | 17/32 | 13.49375 |
| 9/64 | 3.571875 | 35/64 | 13.89063 |
| 5/32 | 3.968750 | 9/16 | 14.28750 |
| 11/64 | 4.365625 | 37/64 | 14.68438 |
| 3/16 | 4.762500 | 19/32 | 15.08125 |
| 13/64 | 5.159375 | 39/64 | 15.47813 |
| 7/32 | 5.556250 | 5/8 | 15.87500 |
| 15/64 | 5.953125 | 41/64 | 16.27188 |
| 1/4 | 6.350000 | 21/32 | 16.66875 |
| 17/64 | 6.746875 | 43/64 | 17.06563 |
| 9/32 | 7.143750 | 11/16 | 17.46250 |
| 19/64 | 7.540625 | 45/64 | 17.85938 |
| 5/16 | 7.937500 | 23/32 | 18.25625 |
| 21/64 | 8.334375 | 47/64 | 18.65313 |
| 11/32 | 8.731250 | 3/4 | 19.05000 |
| 23/64 | 9.128125 | 49/64 | 19.44688 |
| 3/8 | 9.525000 | 25/32 | 19.84375 |
| 25/64 | 9.921875 | 51/64 | 20.24063 |
| 13/32 | 10.31875 | 13/16 | 20.63750 |

| Inches (Fraction) | Millimeters (Decimal Equivalent) |
|---|---|
| 53/64 | 21.03438 |
| 27/32 | 21.43125 |
| 55/64 | 21.82813 |
| 7/8 | 22.22500 |
| 57/64 | 22.62188 |
| 29/32 | 23.01875 |
| 59/64 | 23.41563 |
| 15/16 | 23.81250 |
| 61/64 | 24.20938 |
| 31/32 | 24.60625 |
| 63/64 | 25.00313 |
| 1 | 25.40000 |

## U. S. Weights and Measures

### Length
Mil = .001 inch
1000 mils = 1 inch = .083333 foot
12 inches = 1 foot = .33333 yard
3 feet = 1 yard = 36 inches
5½ yards = 1 rod = 16½ feet

### Square Measure (Area)
1 square inch = .00694 square foot =
    .00077 square yard
144 square inches = 1 square foot =
    .11111 square yard
9 square feet = 1 square yard =
    1296 square inches
30¼ square yards = 1 square rod = .00625 acre

### Cubic Measure (Volume)
1 cubic inch = .00058 cubic foot =
    .00002 cubic yard
1728 cubic inches = 1 cubic foot =
    .03704 cubic yard
27 cubic feet = 1 cubic yard =
    46,656 cubic yards
128 cubic feet = 1 cord = 4.736 cubic yards

### Capacity—Liquid Measure
60 minims = 1 fluidram = .22559 cubic inch
8 fluidrams = 1 fluid ounce =
    1.80469 cubic inches
4 fluid ounces = 1 gill = 7.21875 cubic inches
4 gills = 1 pint = 28.875 cubic inches
2 pints = 1 quart = 57.75 cubic inches
4 quarts = 1 gallon = 231 cubic inches
31½ gallons = 1 barrel = 7277 cubic inches

## Capacity—Dry Measure

1 pint = ½ quart = 33.6 cubic inches
2 pints = 1 quart = 67.2 cubic inches
8 quarts = 1 peck = 537.6 cubic inches
4 pecks = 1 bushel = 2150.4 cubic inches

## Weight (Avoirdupois)

27.344 grains = 1 dram = .0625 ounce
16 drams = 1 ounce = 437.5 grains
16 ounces = 1 pound = 7000 grains
25 pounds = 1 quarter = 400 ounces
100 pounds = 1 short hundredweight = .05 short ton
112 pounds = 1 long hundredweight = .05 long ton
20 short hundredweight = 1 short ton = 2000 pounds
20 long hundredweight = 1 long ton = 2240 pounds

## Metric Weights and Measures

### Length

1 millimeter = .001 meter
10 millimeters = 1 centimeter = .01 meter
10 centimeters = 1 decimeter = .10 meter
10 decimeters = 1 meter
10 meters = 1 dekameter
10 dekameters = 1 hectometer = 100 meters
10 hectometers = 1 kilometer = 1000 meters

### Square Measure (Area)

100 square millimeters = 1 square centimeter = .0001 square meter
100 square centimeters = 1 square decimeter = .01 square meter
100 square decimeters = 1 square meter
100 square meters = 1 square dekameter
100 square dekameters = 1 square hectometer = 10,000 square meters

## Cubic Measure (Volume)

1000 cubic millimeters = 1 cubic centimeter = .000001 cubic meter
1000 cubic centimeters = 1 cubic decimeter = .001 cubic meter
1000 cubic decimeters = 1 cubic meter

## Capacity

10 millimeters = 1 centiliter = .01 liter
10 centiliters = 1 deciliter = .10 liter
10 deciliters = 1 liter
10 liters = 1 dekaliter
10 dekaliters = 1 hectoliter = 100 liters
10 hectoliters = 1 kiloliter = 1000 liters

## Weight

10 milligrams = 1 centigram = .01 gram
10 centigrams = 1 decigram = .10 gram
10 decigrams = 1 gram
10 grams = 1 dekagram
10 dekagrams = 1 hectogram = 100 grams
10 hectograms = 1 kilogram = 1000 grams
100 kilograms = 1 quintal = 100,000 grams
10 quintals = 1 ton = 1,000,000 grams

## U. S. and Metric Equivalents

### Length

1 inch = 25.4 millimeters = 2.54 centimeters = .0254 meter
1 foot = 304.80 millimeters = 30.48 centimeters = .3048 meter
1 yard = 914.40 millimeters = 91.44 centimeters = .9144 meter
1 millimeter = .03937 inch = .00328083 foot = .00109361 yard
1 centimeter = .39370 inch = .03280830 foot = .01093610 yard
1 meter = 39.37 inches = 3.28083 feet = 1.093611 yards

## Square Measure (Area)

1 square inch = 645.16 square millimeters =
6.4516 square centimeters =
.00064516 square meter

1 square foot = 92,903 square millimeters =
929.03 square centimeters =
.092903 square meter

1 square yard = 836,127 square millimeters =
8361.27 square centimeters =
.836127 square meter

1 square millimeter = .0015499 square inch

1 square centimeter = .154999 square inch =
.001076 square foot

1 square meter = 1549.99 square inches =
10.7638 square feet =
1.19599 square yards

## Cubic Measure (Volume)

1 cubic inch = 16,387 cubic millimeters =
16.3871 cubic centimeters

1 cubic foot = 28,317 cubic centimeters =
.0283168 cubic meter

1 cubic yard = .7645548 cubic meter

1 cubic millimeter = .000061 cubic inch

1 cubic centimeter = .06102 cubic inch

1 cubic meter = 35.314 cubic feet =
1.3079 cubic yards

## Capacity

1 minim = .061610 milliliter = .0000616 liter

1 fluidram = 3.6967 millliters = .0036967 liter

1 fluid ounce = 29.5729 millilters =
.0295729 liter

1 gill = 118.294 milliliters = .118294 liter

1 pint (liquid) = 473.176 milliliters = .473176 liter

1 quart (liquid) = 946.35 milliliters = .94635 liter

1 gallon (liquid) = 3785.4 milliliters = 3.7854 liters

1 milliliter = .27 fluidram = .06102 cubic inch

1 centiliter = .338 fluid ounce =
.61020 cubic inches

1 deciliter = .21 pint (liquid) =
6.1020 cubic inches

1 liter = 1.057 quarts (liquid) =
61.020 cubic inches

1 dekaliter = 2.64 gallons (liquid) = 609.840 cubic
inches

## Weight

1 grain = .0648 gram

1 dram (avoirdupois) = 1.77185 grams

1 ounce (avoirdupois) = 28.3495 grams

1 pound (avoirdupois) = .4536 kilogram

1 short hundredweight = 45.359 kilograms

1 long hundredweight = 50.848 kilograms

1 short ton = .90718 metric ton

1 long ton = 1.0161 metric tons

## Conversion Table

Note: British imperial measure (liquid and dry) is not shown. The British imperial gallon equals 1.2009 U.S. gallons.

| To Convert From: | To: | Multiply By: |
|---|---|---|
| centigrams | grains | .15432 |
| | grams | .01 |
| centiliters | fluidrams | 2.705 |
| | fluid ounces | .33814 |
| | liters | .01 |
| centimeters | feet | .03281 |
| | inches | .3937 |
| | meters | .01 |
| | mils | 393.7 |
| cubic centimeters | cubic feet | .00003532 |
| | cubic inches | .06102 |
| | liters | .001 |
| | cubic meters | .000001 |
| cubic decimeters | cubic centimeters | 1000 |
| | cubic inches | 61.0237 |
| cubic feet | cubic centimeters | 28,317 |
| | cubic inches | 1728 |
| | cubic yards | .03704 |
| | cubic meters | .02832 |
| | gallons (liquid) | 7.48052 |
| | liters | 28.31687 |
| cubic inches | cubic centimeters | 16.3872 |
| | cubic feet | .000579 |
| | cubic meters | .00001639 |
| | gallons (liquid) | .00433 |
| | liters | .01639 |
| | pints (dry) | .02976 |
| | pints (liquid) | .03463 |
| | quarts (dry) | .01488 |
| | quarts (liquid) | .01732 |
| cubic meters | cubic centimeters | 1,000,000 |
| | cubic feet | 35.314 |
| | cubic inches | 61,023.4 |
| | gallons (liquid) | 264.17 |

| To Convert From: | To: | Multiply By: |
|---|---|---|
| cubic millimeters | cubic centimeters | .001 |
| | cubic inches | .00006 |
| cubic yards | cubic feet | 27 |
| | cubic inches | 46,656 |
| | cubic meters | .7646 |
| cup (liquid) | gallon (liquid) | .0625 |
| | ounce (liquid) | 8 |
| | pint (liquid) | .5 |
| | quart (liquid) | .25 |
| decigrams | grains | 1.5432 |
| | grams | .1 |
| deciliters | fluid ounces | 3.38 |
| | liters | .1 |
| decimeters | inches | 3.937 |
| | meters | .01 |
| dekagrams | grams | 10 |
| | ounces (avoirdupois) | .3527 |
| dekaliters | gallons (liquid) | 2.64 |
| | liters | 10 |
| dekameters | inches | 393.7 |
| | meters | 10 |
| drams (avoirdupois) | ounces (avoirdupois) | .0625 |
| | grains | 27.3437 |
| | grams | 1.7718 |
| drams (liquid) | see fluidrams | |
| feet | centimeters | 30.4801 |
| | inches | 12 |
| | meters | .3048 |
| | yards | .3333 |

## Conversion Table (continued)

| To Convert From: | To: | Multiply By: |
|---|---|---|
| fluid ounces | cubic inches | 1.80469 |
| | cups (liquid) | 0.125 |
| | fluidrams | 8 |
| | gallons (liquid) | .00781 |
| | liters | .02959 |
| | pints (liquid) | .0625 |
| | tablespoons | 2 |
| | teaspoons | 6 |
| fluidrams | cubic inches | .22559 |
| | fluid ounces | .125 |
| | milliliters | 3.69669 |
| | minims | 60 |
| gallons (dry) | cubic feet | .1556 |
| | cubic inches | 268.8 |
| | cubic meters | .0044 |
| gallons (liquid) | cubic feet | .1337 |
| | cubic inches | 231 |
| | cubic meters | .0038 |
| | fluid ounces | 128 |
| | liters | 3.7854 |
| | pints (liquid) | 8 |
| | quarts (liquid) | 4 |
| gills | pints (liquid) | .25 |
| | | |
| grains | drams (avoirdupois) | .03657 |
| | grams | .0648 |
| | milligrams | 64.7989 |
| | ounces (avoirdupois) | .00229 |
| | pounds (avoirdupois) | .00014 |
| grams | grains | 15.432 |
| | kilograms | .001 |
| | milligrams | 1000 |
| | ounces (avoirdupois) | 0.3527 |
| | pounds (avoirdupois) | .0022 |
| hectograms | grams | 100 |
| | ounces (avoirdupois) | 3.5274 |

| To Convert From: | To: | Multiply By: |
|---|---|---|
| hectoliters | gallons (liquid) | 26.418 |
|  | liters | 100 |
| inches | centimeters | 2.54 |
|  | feet | .08333 |
|  | meters | .0254 |
|  | millimeters | 25.4 |
|  | mils | 1000 |
|  | yards | .02778 |
| kilograms | grains | 15,432.36 |
|  | grams | 1000 |
|  | ounces (avoirdupois) | 35.274 |
|  | pounds (avoirdupois) | 2.2046 |
| kiloliters | gallons (liquid) | 264.172 |
|  | liters | 1000 |
| kilometers | feet | 3280.833 |
|  | meters | 1000 |
| liters | cubic centimeters | 1000 |
|  | cubic feet | .035313 |
|  | cubic inches | 61.02398 |
|  | quarts (dry) | .9081 |
|  | quarts (liquid) | 1.0567 |
|  | gallons (dry) | .22702 |
|  | gallons (liquid) | .26417 |
| long tons | pounds (avoirdupois) | 2240 |
| meters | feet | 3.2808 |
|  | inches | 39.37 |
|  | kilometers | .001 |
|  | millimeters | 1000 |
| microinches | inches | .000001 |
|  | centimeters | .0001 |
|  | microns | .0254 |
| microns | inches | .0000394 |
|  | meters | .000001 |
|  | microinches | 37.370079 |
|  | mils | .03937 |

## Conversion Table (continued)

| To Convert From: | To: | Multiply By: |
|---|---|---|
| milligrams | grains | .01543 |
| | grams | .001 |
| milliliters | fluid ounces | .0338 |
| | fluidrams | .2705 |
| | liters | .001 |
| millimeters | inches | .03937 |
| | meters | .001 |
| | microns | 1000 |
| | mils | 39.37 |
| mils | inches | .001 |
| | microns | 25.4001 |
| | millimeters | .0254 |
| minims | fluidrams | .01667 |
| | milliliters | .06161 |
| ounces (avoirdupois) | drams (avoirdupois) | 16 |
| | grains | 437.5 |
| | grams | 28.350 |
| | pounds (avoirdupois) | .0625 |
| ounces (liquid) | see fluid ounces | |
| pints (dry) | cubic inches | 33.6003 |
| | liters | .5506 |
| | quarts (dry) | .5 |
| pints (liquid) | cubic inches | 28.875 |
| | cups (liquid) | 2 |
| | fluid ounces | 16 |
| | gallons (liquid) | .125 |
| | quarts (liquid) | .5 |
| | gills | 4 |
| | liters | .47318 |
| pounds (avoirdupois) | grams | 453.592 |
| | grains | 7000 |
| | ounces (avoirdupois) | 16 |
| quarts (dry) | cubic inches | 67.2006 |
| | liters | 1.10112 |
| | pints (dry) | 2 |

| To Convert From: | To: | Multiply By: |
| --- | --- | --- |
| quarts (liquid) | cubic inches<br>gallons (liquid)<br>liters<br>pints (liquid) | 57.75<br>.25<br>.94636<br>2 |
| square centimeters | square feet<br>square inches<br>square millimeters | .001076<br>.1550<br>100 |
| square decimeters | square inches<br>square meters | 15.5<br>.01 |
| square dekameters | square meters<br>square yards | 100<br>119.599 |
| square feet | square centimeters<br>square inches<br>square meters<br>square yards | 929.0341<br>144<br>.0929<br>.1111 |
| square hectometers | square meters | 10,000 |
| square inches | square centimeters<br>square feet<br>square millimeters<br>square yards | 6.4515<br>.00694<br>645.1625<br>.00077 |
| square meters | square centimeters<br>square feet<br>square yards | 10,000<br>10.7639<br>1.196 |
| square millimeters | square inches<br>square meters | .00155<br>.000001 |
| square yards | square feet<br>square inches<br>square meters | 9<br>1296<br>.83613 |
| tablespoon (liquid) | teaspoon (liquid) | 3 |
| teaspoon (liquid) | fluid ounce<br>tablespoon (liquid) | .166666<br>.333333 |
| yards | feet<br>inches<br>meters | 3<br>36<br>.9144 |

## Table of Powers and Roots

| Fraction (In Lowest Terms) or Whole Number | Decimal Equivalent | Square | Cube | Square Root | Cube Root |
|---|---|---|---|---|---|
| 1/64 | .015625 | .0002441 | .000003815 | .125 | .25 |
| 1/32 | .03125 | .0009766 | .000030518 | .176777 | .31498 |
| 3/64 | .046875 | .0021973 | .000102997 | .216506 | .36056 |
| 1/16 | .0625 | .0039063 | .00024414 | .25 | .39685 |
| 5/64 | .078125 | .0061035 | .00047684 | .279508 | .42749 |
| 3/32 | .09375 | .0087891 | .00082398 | .306186 | .45428 |
| 7/64 | .109375 | .0119629 | .0013084 | .330719 | .47823 |
| 1/8 | .125 | .0156250 | .0019531 | .353553 | .5 |
| 9/64 | .140625 | .0197754 | .0027809 | .375 | .52002 |
| 5/32 | .15625 | .0244141 | .0038147 | .395285 | .53861 |
| 11/64 | .171875 | .0295410 | .0050774 | .414578 | .55600 |
| 3/16 | .1875 | .0351563 | .0065918 | .433013 | .57236 |
| 13/64 | .203125 | .0412598 | .0083809 | .450694 | .58783 |
| 7/32 | .21875 | .0478516 | .010468 | .467707 | .60254 |
| 15/64 | .234375 | .0549316 | .012875 | .484123 | .61655 |
| 1/4 | .25 | .0625 | .015625 | .5 | .62996 |
| 17/64 | .265625 | .0705566 | .018742 | .515388 | .64282 |
| 9/32 | .28125 | .0791016 | .022247 | .530330 | .65519 |
| 19/64 | .296875 | .0881348 | .026165 | .544862 | .66710 |
| 5/16 | .3125 | .0976562 | .030518 | .559017 | .67860 |
| 21/64 | .328125 | .107666 | .035328 | .572822 | .68973 |
| 11/32 | .34375 | .118164 | .040619 | .586302 | .70051 |
| 23/64 | .359375 | .129150 | .046413 | .599479 | .71097 |
| 3/8 | .375 | .140625 | .052734 | .612372 | .72113 |
| 25/64 | .390625 | .1525879 | .059605 | .625 | .73100 |
| 13/32 | .40625 | .1650391 | .067047 | .637377 | .74062 |

| Fraction (In Lowest Terms) or Whole Number | Decimal Equivalent | Square | Cube | Square Root | Cube Root |
|---|---|---|---|---|---|
| 27/64 | .421875 | .1779785 | .075085 | .649519 | .75 |
| 7/16 | .4375 | .1914063 | .083740 | .661438 | .75915 |
| 29/64 | .453125 | .2053223 | .093037 | .673146 | .76808 |
| 15/32 | .46875 | .2197266 | .102997 | .684653 | .77681 |
| 31/64 | .484375 | .2346191 | .113644 | .695971 | .78535 |
| 1/2 | .5 | .25 | .125 | .707107 | .79370 |
| 33/64 | .515625 | .265869 | .137089 | .718070 | .80188 |
| 17/32 | .53125 | .282227 | .149933 | .728869 | .80990 |
| 35/64 | .546875 | .299072 | .163555 | .739510 | .81777 |
| 9/16 | .5625 | .316406 | .177979 | .75 | .82548 |
| 37/64 | .578125 | .334229 | .193226 | .760345 | .83306 |
| 19/32 | .59375 | .352539 | .209320 | .770552 | .84049 |
| 39/64 | .609375 | .371338 | .226284 | .780625 | .84780 |
| 5/8 | .625 | .390625 | .244141 | .790569 | .85499 |
| 41/64 | .640625 | .410400 | .262913 | .800391 | .86205 |
| 21/32 | .65625 | .430664 | .282623 | .810093 | .86901 |
| 43/64 | .671875 | .451416 | .303295 | .819680 | .87585 |
| 11/16 | .6875 | .472656 | .324951 | .829156 | .88259 |
| 45/64 | .703125 | .494385 | .347614 | .838525 | .88922 |
| 23/32 | .71875 | .516602 | .371307 | .847791 | .89576 |
| 47/64 | .734375 | .539307 | .396053 | .856957 | .90221 |
| 3/4 | .75 | .5625 | .421875 | .866025 | .90856 |
| 49/64 | .765625 | .586182 | .448795 | .875 | .91483 |
| 25/32 | .78125 | .610352 | .476837 | .883883 | .92101 |
| 51/64 | .796875 | .635010 | .506023 | .892679 | .92711 |
| 13/16 | .8125 | .660156 | .536377 | .901388 | .93313 |

## Table of Powers and Roots (continued)

| Fraction (In Lowest Terms) or Whole Number | Decimal Equivalent | Square | Cube | Square Root | Cube Root |
|---|---|---|---|---|---|
| 53/64 | .828125 | .685791 | .567921 | .910014 | .93907 |
| 27/32 | .84375 | .711914 | .600677 | .918559 | .94494 |
| 55/64 | .859375 | .738525 | .634670 | .927025 | .95074 |
| 7/8 | .875 | .765625 | .669922 | .935414 | .95647 |
| 57/64 | .890625 | .793213 | .706455 | .943729 | .96213 |
| 29/32 | .90625 | .821289 | .744293 | .951972 | .96772 |
| 59/64 | .921875 | .849854 | .783459 | .960143 | .97325 |
| 15/16 | .9375 | .878906 | .823975 | .968246 | .97872 |
| 61/64 | .953125 | .908447 | .865864 | .976281 | .98412 |
| 31/32 | .96875 | .938477 | .909149 | .984251 | .98947 |
| 63/64 | .984375 | .968994 | .953854 | .992157 | .99476 |
| 1 | 1.000000 | 1 | 1 | 1.00000 | 1.00000 |
| 2 | 2.000000 | 4 | 8 | 1.41421 | 1.25992 |
| 3 | 3.000000 | 9 | 27 | 1.73205 | 1.44225 |
| 4 | 4.000000 | 16 | 64 | 2.00000 | 1.58740 |
| 5 | 5.000000 | 25 | 125 | 2.23607 | 1.70998 |
| 6 | 6.000000 | 36 | 216 | 2.44949 | 1.81712 |
| 7 | 7.000000 | 49 | 343 | 2.64575 | 1.91293 |
| 8 | 8.000000 | 64 | 512 | 2.82843 | 2.00000 |
| 9 | 9.000000 | 81 | 729 | 3.00000 | 2.08008 |
| 10 | 10.000000 | 100 | 1000 | 3.16228 | 2.15443 |
| 11 | 11.000000 | 121 | 1331 | 3.31662 | 2.22398 |
| 12 | 12.000000 | 144 | 1728 | 3.46410 | 2.28943 |
| 13 | 13.000000 | 169 | 2197 | 3.60555 | 2.35133 |
| 14 | 14.000000 | 196 | 2744 | 3.74166 | 2.41014 |
| 15 | 15.000000 | 225 | 3375 | 3.87298 | 2.46621 |

| Fraction (In Lowest Terms) or Whole Number | Decimal Equivalent | Square | Cube | Square Root | Cube Root |
|---|---|---|---|---|---|
| 16 | 16.000000 | 256 | 4096 | 4.00000 | 2.51984 |
| 17 | 17.000000 | 289 | 4913 | 4.12311 | 2.57128 |
| 18 | 18.000000 | 324 | 5832 | 4.24264 | 2.62074 |
| 19 | 19.000000 | 361 | 6859 | 4.35890 | 2.66840 |
| 20 | 20.000000 | 400 | 8000 | 4.47214 | 2.71442 |
| 21 | 21.000000 | 441 | 9261 | 4.58258 | 2.75892 |
| 22 | 22.000000 | 484 | 10,648 | 4.69042 | 2.80204 |
| 23 | 23.000000 | 529 | 12,167 | 4.79583 | 2.84387 |
| 24 | 24.000000 | 576 | 13,824 | 4.89898 | 2.88450 |
| 25 | 25.000000 | 625 | 15,625 | 5.00000 | 2.92402 |
| 26 | 26.000000 | 676 | 17,576 | 5.09902 | 2.96250 |
| 27 | 27.000000 | 729 | 19,683 | 5.19615 | 3.00000 |
| 28 | 28.000000 | 784 | 21,952 | 5.29150 | 3.03659 |
| 29 | 29.000000 | 841 | 24,389 | 5.38516 | 3.07232 |
| 30 | 30.000000 | 900 | 27,000 | 5.47723 | 3.10723 |
| 31 | 31.000000 | 961 | 29,791 | 5.56776 | 3.14138 |
| 32 | 32.000000 | 1024 | 32,768 | 5.65685 | 3.17480 |
| 33 | 33.000000 | 1089 | 35,937 | 5.74456 | 3.20753 |
| 34 | 34.000000 | 1156 | 39,304 | 5.83095 | 3.23961 |
| 35 | 35.000000 | 1225 | 42,875 | 5.91608 | 3.27107 |
| 36 | 36.000000 | 1296 | 46,656 | 6.00000 | 3.30193 |
| 37 | 37.000000 | 1369 | 50,653 | 6.08276 | 3.33222 |
| 38 | 38.000000 | 1444 | 54,872 | 6.16441 | 3.36198 |
| 39 | 39.000000 | 1521 | 59,319 | 6.24500 | 3.39121 |
| 40 | 40.000000 | 1600 | 64,000 | 6.32456 | 3.41995 |
| 41 | 41.000000 | 1681 | 68,921 | 6.40312 | 3.44822 |

## Table of Powers and Roots (continued)

| Fraction (In Lowest Terms) or Whole Number | Decimal Equivalent | Square | Cube | Square Root | Cube Root |
|---|---|---|---|---|---|
| 42 | 42.000000 | 1764 | 74,088 | 6.48074 | 3.47603 |
| 43 | 43.000000 | 1849 | 79,507 | 6.55744 | 3.50340 |
| 44 | 44.000000 | 1936 | 85,184 | 6.63325 | 3.53035 |
| 45 | 45.000000 | 2025 | 91,125 | 6.70820 | 3.55689 |
| 46 | 46.000000 | 2116 | 97,336 | 6.78233 | 3.58305 |
| 47 | 47.000000 | 2209 | 103,823 | 6.85565 | 3.60883 |
| 48 | 48.000000 | 2304 | 110,592 | 6.92820 | 3.63424 |
| 49 | 49.000000 | 2401 | 117,649 | 7.00000 | 3.65931 |
| 50 | 50.000000 | 2500 | 125,000 | 7.07107 | 3.68403 |
| 51 | 51.000000 | 2601 | 132,651 | 7.14143 | 3.70843 |
| 52 | 52.000000 | 2704 | 140,608 | 7.21110 | 3.73251 |
| 53 | 53.000000 | 2809 | 148,877 | 7.28011 | 3.75629 |
| 54 | 54.000000 | 2916 | 157,464 | 7.34847 | 3.77976 |
| 55 | 55.000000 | 3025 | 166,375 | 7.41620 | 3.80295 |
| 56 | 56.000000 | 3136 | 175,616 | 7.48331 | 3.82586 |
| 57 | 57.000000 | 3249 | 185,193 | 7.54983 | 3.84850 |
| 58 | 58.000000 | 3364 | 195,112 | 7.61577 | 3.87088 |
| 59 | 59.000000 | 3481 | 205,379 | 7.68115 | 3.89300 |
| 60 | 60.000000 | 3600 | 216,000 | 7.74597 | 3.91487 |
| 61 | 61.000000 | 3721 | 226,981 | 7.81025 | 3.93650 |
| 62 | 62.000000 | 3844 | 238,328 | 7.87401 | 3.95789 |
| 63 | 63.000000 | 3969 | 250,047 | 7.93725 | 3.97906 |
| 64 | 64.000000 | 4096 | 262,144 | 8.00000 | 4.00000 |
| 65 | 65.000000 | 4225 | 274,625 | 8.06226 | 4.02073 |
| 66 | 66.000000 | 4356 | 287,496 | 8.12404 | 4.04124 |
| 67 | 67.000000 | 4489 | 300,763 | 8.18535 | 4.06155 |

| Fraction (In Lowest Terms) or Whole Number | Decimal Equivalent | Square | Cube | Square Root | Cube Root |
|---|---|---|---|---|---|
| 68 | 68.000000 | 4624 | 314,432 | 8.24621 | 4.08166 |
| 69 | 69.000000 | 4761 | 328,509 | 8.30662 | 4.10157 |
| 70 | 70.000000 | 4900 | 343,000 | 8.36660 | 4.12129 |
| 71 | 71.000000 | 5041 | 357,911 | 8.42615 | 4.14082 |
| 72 | 72.000000 | 5184 | 373,248 | 8.48528 | 4.16017 |
| 73 | 73.000000 | 5329 | 389,017 | 8.54400 | 4.17934 |
| 74 | 74.000000 | 5476 | 405,224 | 8.60233 | 4.19834 |
| 75 | 75.000000 | 5625 | 421,875 | 8.66025 | 4.21716 |
| 76 | 76.000000 | 5776 | 438,976 | 8.71780 | 4.23582 |
| 77 | 77.000000 | 5929 | 456,533 | 8.77496 | 4.25432 |
| 78 | 78.000000 | 6084 | 474,552 | 8.83176 | 4.27266 |
| 79 | 79.000000 | 6241 | 493,039 | 8.88819 | 4.29084 |
| 80 | 80.000000 | 6400 | 512,000 | 8.94427 | 4.30887 |
| 81 | 81.000000 | 6561 | 531,441 | 9.00000 | 4.32675 |
| 82 | 82.000000 | 6724 | 551,368 | 9.05539 | 4.34448 |
| 83 | 83.000000 | 6889 | 571,787 | 9.11043 | 4.36207 |
| 84 | 84.000000 | 7056 | 592,704 | 9.16515 | 4.37952 |
| 85 | 85.000000 | 7225 | 614,125 | 9.21954 | 4.39683 |
| 86 | 86.000000 | 7396 | 636,056 | 9.27362 | 4.41400 |
| 87 | 87.000000 | 7569 | 658,503 | 9.32738 | 4.43105 |
| 88 | 88.000000 | 7744 | 681,472 | 9.38083 | 4.44796 |
| 89 | 89.000000 | 7921 | 704,969 | 9.43398 | 4.46475 |
| 90 | 90.000000 | 8100 | 729,000 | 9.48683 | 4.48140 |
| 91 | 91.000000 | 8281 | 753,571 | 9.53939 | 4.49794 |
| 92 | 92.000000 | 8464 | 778,688 | 9.59166 | 4.51436 |
| 93 | 93.000000 | 8649 | 804,357 | 9.64365 | 4.53065 |

## Table of Powers and Roots (continued)

| Fraction (In Lowest Terms) or Whole Number | Decimal Equivalent | Square | Cube | Square Root | Cube Root |
|---|---|---|---|---|---|
| 94 | 94.000000 | 8836 | 830,584 | 9.69536 | 4.54684 |
| 95 | 95.000000 | 9025 | 857,375 | 9.74679 | 4.56290 |
| 96 | 96.000000 | 9216 | 884,736 | 9.79796 | 4.57886 |
| 97 | 97.000000 | 9409 | 912,673 | 9.84886 | 4.59470 |
| 98 | 98.000000 | 9604 | 941,192 | 9.89949 | 4.61044 |
| 99 | 99.000000 | 9801 | 970,299 | 9.94987 | 4.62607 |
| 100 | 100.000000 | 10,000 | 1,000,000 | 10.00000 | 4.64159 |

## About the Author

Tom Begnal is a life-long woodworker whose interest in the craft evolved into a full-time furniture business in northwestern Connecticut. He moved on to become the managing editor of *The Woodworker's Journal* magazine for more than fifteen years and eventually joined the editorial staff at *Shopnotes* in Des Moines, Iowa. His final stop was as an associate editor at *Fine Woodworking* magazine. He has also written or edited woodworking and how-to books for several publishers including F+W Publications, McGraw-Hill, Rodale Press and Sterling Publishing. Now retired, Tom lives in Connecticut.

## Dedication

To my remarkable children: Colleen, Kevin and Brendan

# *Index*

for temperature conversion, 139–40

volume, 82–83

woodshop applications, 126, 127, 129, 130, 134–35, 136, 137, 140, 141–42, 146

fractions. *See also* ratios and proportions

about: overview of, 9

adding, 18–22

cancelling, 25

changing decimals to, 36–37

changing to decimals, 37, 50–51

common denominators, 12–14

components of, 9

decimals and, 32, 36–37. *See also* decimals

defined, 9

denominator defined, 9

dividing, 10, 27–29

equivalent, 12

fraction line/bar defined, 9

improper, 10, 16–17

like fractions, 14

lowest common denominator, 13–14

mixed numbers, 16–17

multiplying, 24–27

numerator defined, 9

powers and, 54

proper, 10

raising to higher terms, 12

reading, 9–10

reducing to lowest terms, 10–11

roots as, 57, 184–90

subtracting, 22–24

types of, 10–11

unlike fractions, 15

whole numbers as, 12

woodshop application, 30–31

**G**

geometry. *See also* plane figures; polygons; *specific shapes*

angles and. *See* angles

basic theorems of, 98–101

lines and. *See* lines

solid figures, 71–75. *See also* cones; cylinders; prisms; pyramids; spheres

glossary of terms, 165–69

Golden Rectangle, 157–58

grid patterns, enlarging, 103–8

about: overview of, 103

grid square method, 103–6

photocopy method, 106–8

**H**

hearts, drawing, 97

hexagons, regular. *See also* polygons

area formula, 78

defined, 67

drawing, 90

perimeter formula, 78

hexahedrons. *See* prisms

**J**

jointer feed-rate chart, 138

jointer-cutterhead-speed formulas, 138–39

**L**

lines

basic theorems about intersections of, 98

bisecting, 85–86

trisecting, 86

types of, 61–62

load (shelf), calculating, 130–35

**M**

measurements. *See also* conversions

calipers for, 159, 161–63

micrometers for, 159–61

micrometers, reading, 159–61

miter angles, determining, 127–29

MOE (modulus of elasticity), 131

moisture content of wood, determining, 125–26

movement of wood, calculating, 147–52

multiplying

cross product rule, 153–54

decimals, 44–46

fractions, 24–27

powers, 55–56

# MORE GREAT BOOKS *from*
# SPRING HOUSE PRESS

**Classic Wooden Toys**
978-1-940611-34-1
$24.95 | 176 Pages

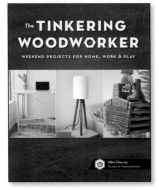

**The Tinkering Woodworker**
978-1-940611-08-2
$24.95 | 152 Pages

**Getting Started in Woodturning**
978-1-940611-09-9
$27.95 | 224 Pages

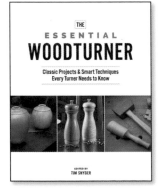

**The Essential Woodturner**
978-1-940611-47-1
$27.95 | 228 Pages

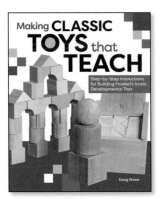

**Making Classic Toys That Teach**
978-1-940611-33-4
$24.95 | 144 Pages

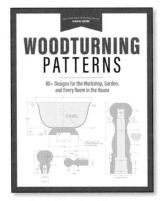

**Woodturning Patterns**
978-1-940611-69-3
$22.95 | 144 Pages

**SPRING HOUSE PRESS**

Look for these Spring House Press titles at your favorite bookstore, specialty retailer, or visit *www.springhousepress.com.*
For more information about Spring House Press, call 1-717-569-5196 or email us at *info@springhousepress.com.*

# MORE GREAT BOOKS *from*
# SPRING HOUSE PRESS

## *The Illustrated Workshop Series*

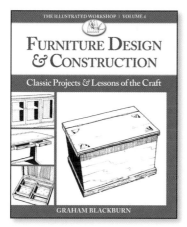

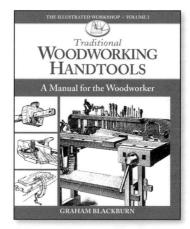

**Furniture Design & Construction**
978-1-940611-05-1
$24.95 | 256 Pages

**The Illustrated Encyclopedia of
Handtools, Instruments & Devices**
978-1-940611-02-0
$24.95 | 206 Pages

**Traditional Woodworking
Handtools**
978-1-940611-03-7
$29.95 | 384 Pages

SPRING HOUSE PRESS

Look for these Spring House Press titles at your favorite bookstore, specialty retailer, or visit *www.springhousepress.com.*
For more information about Spring House Press, call 1-717-569-5196 or email us at *info@springhousepress.com.*

# MORE GREAT BOOKS *from*
# SPRING HOUSE PRESS

WITHDRAWN

**The Minimalist Woodworker**
978-1-940611-35-8
$24.95 | 152 Pages

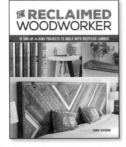

**The Reclaimed Woodworker**
978-1-940611-54-9
$24.95 | 168 Pages

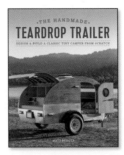

**The Box Maker's Guitar Book**
978-1-940611-64-8
$24.95 | 168 Pages

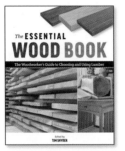

**The Essential Wood Book**
978-1-940611-37-2
$27.95 | 216 Pages

**The Handmade Teardrop Trailer**
978-1-940611-65-5
$27.00 | 224 Pages

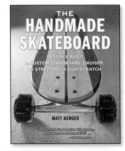

**The Handmade Skateboard**
978-1-940611-06-8
$24.95 | 160 Pages

**Make Your Own Knife Handles**
978-1-940611-53-2
$22.95 | 168 Pages

**Make Your Own Cutting Boards**
978-1-940611-45-7
$22.95 | 168 Pages

**The New Bandsaw Box Book**
978-1-940611-32-7
$19.95 | 120 Pages

SPRING HOUSE PRESS

Look for these Spring House Press titles at your favorite bookstore, specialty retailer, or visit *www.springhousepress.com*.
For more information about Spring House Press, call 1-717-569-5196 or email us at *info@springhousepress.com*.